NEW YORK STATE Coach

America's Best for Student Success

English Language Arts

GRADE **6**

Content Development by
Triple SSS Press Media Development

New York State Coach, English Language Arts, Grade 6
78NY
ISBN: 1-58620-924-8

EVP, Product Development: Bill Scroggie
VP, Creative Director: Spencer Brinker
VP of Production: Dina Goren
Executive Editor: Adriana Velez
Art Director: Farzana Razak

Senior Development Editor: Justin Trewartha
Development Editor: Max Winter
Author: Triple SSS Press Media Development
Graphic Designer: Lauren Kampel

Cover Design: Farzana Razak
Cover Photo: Lloyd Birmingham/Images.com

Triumph Learning® 136 Madison Avenue, 7th Floor, New York, NY 10016
© 2005 Triumph Learning, LLC
A Haights Cross Communications® company

Printed in the United States of America.

10 9 8 7 6 5 4 3 2

Table of Contents

New York State English Language Arts
Standards

Standard	Lesson	Description
Standard 1		
S1.I.1.A	12, 13, 14	interpret and analyze information from textbooks and nonfiction books for young adults, as well as reference materials, audio and media presentations, oral interviews, graphs, charts, diagrams, and electronic data bases intended for a general audience
S1.I.1.B	12, 13, 14, 15	compare and synthesize information from different sources
S1.I.1.D	22, 23	distinguish between relevant and irrelevant information and between fact and opinion
S1.I.1.E	20, 24	relate new information to prior knowledge and experience
S1.I.1.F	16, 17, 18, 19, 20	understand and use the text features that make information accessible and usable, such as format, sequence, level of diction, and relevance of details
S1.I.2.A	28, 29 30, 31	produce oral and written reports on topics related to all school subjects
S1.I.2.B	32	establish an authoritative stance on the subject and provide references to establish the validity and verifiability of the information presented
S1.I.2.C	25, 26, 27	organize information according to an identifiable structure, such as compare/contrast or general to specific
S1.I.2.E	28, 29, 30, 31	use the process of prewriting, drafting, revising, and proofreading (the "writing process") to produce well-constructed informational texts
S1.I.2.F	39, 40, 41, 42, 43, 44, 45	use standard English for formal presentation of information, selecting appropriate grammatical constructions and vocabulary, using a variety of sentence structures and observing the rules of punctuation, capitalization, and spelling
Standard 2		
S2.I.1.A	1	read and view texts and performances from a wide range of authors, subjects, and genres
S2.I.1.B	1	understand and identify the distinguishing features of the major genres and use them to aid their interpretation and discussion of literature
S2.I.1.C	2, 3, 4, 5, 6, 7, 8, 9, 21	identify significant literary elements (including metaphor, symbolism, foreshadowing, dialect, rhyme, meter, irony, climax) and use those elements to interpret the work
S2.I.1.D	7	recognize different levels of meaning
S2.I.2.C	10, 11	write stories, poems, literary essays, and plays that observe the conventions of the genre and contain interesting and effective language and voice
S2.I.2.D	10, 11	use standard English effectively
Standard 3		
S3.I.1.A	12	analyze, interpret, and evaluate information, ideas, organization, and language from academic and nonacademic texts, such as textbooks, public documents, book and movie reviews, and editorials
S3.I.2.A	33, 34, 35	present (in essays, position papers, speeches, and debates) clear analyses of issues, ideas, texts, and experiences, supporting their positions with well-developed arguments

Introduction

Every year, New York State administers an English Language Arts test, which is used to determine what students have learned in reading and writing.

This test does <u>not</u> test how many reading and writing details students have memorized. It is a test of how well they understand some of the important ideas and skills necessary to be good readers and writers.

This book, the **New York State Coach, English Language Arts, Grade 6** was written to help student sharpen their English Language Arts skills and prepare for the test in the following ways.

The **Coach** consists of units that are divided into chapters and lessons, following a structure based on the New York State English Language Arts Standards. Every lesson focuses on teaching a single skill within a *Standard*. After instructing on the *Standard* or *Anchor*, the lesson provides a *Thinking It Through* question, which is a short answer question pertaining to the lesson's skill. The lessons also provides example questions. Each of these is followed by a *Quick Coach* which helps students understand how to answer the question. The last *Example* question tells the student that the teacher will go over their answer with them. Finally, the regularly occurring *Test Practice* sections give opportunities to review and ask test-like questions to test what students have learned.

Students work through the book carefully, remembering that the concept, or "big idea," behind an answer is more important than the answer itself. There are no shortcuts to doing well on the New York State English/Language Arts test. Students should study hard and let the **New York State Coach, English Language Arts, Grade 6** guide them to success.

To the Student

Each year, New York State gives students like you something called the **NYS English Language Arts** test. This test shows just how much you've learned about reading and writing in sixth grade. So how do you get ready for this test? With this book: the ***NYS English Language Arts Coach, Grade 6***.

Each chapter of this book teaches you an important skill on the test. And each chapter gives you lots of opportunities to understand and practice that skill. To make sure you make the most of these opportunities and are as ready as you can be for the test— here's what you should do with this book:

- Read every chapter and lesson. Don't skip anything. Once you read and understand all the chapters, you'll know what you need to for the test.

- Answer all the *Thinking It Through, Example, Coached Reading*, and *Test Practice* questions in each chapter. These are the kinds of questions you'll see on the test, so they're a great way to practice. Most of these questions are multiple choice with four possible answers. If more than one answer seems right, always choose the one that <u>best</u> answers the question. If you read the stories and passages in this book carefully, and think carefully while you do so, you'll usually have a good idea which answer is right.

- Listen carefully to the directions your teacher gives you.

Most of all, enjoy the things you're reading and writing. These are skills you'll get to use your whole life.

And good luck on the test. You'll do great!

To the Parent or Caregiver

This book, **New York State Coach, English Language Arts, Grade 6,** helps prepare your child for the **New York State English Language Arts** exam, which New York State gives all sixth-grade students each year.

To help your child prepare and do well on the test, review all the lessons in this book with him or her. Your child's teacher will review all this material in class as well, but your support at home is vital to your child's success.

Encourage your child to read and study this book at home, and take time to review the sample questions with him or her. The more your child practices, the better he or she is likely to do on the test.

As you know, parents and teachers working together can help the students succeed. Thank you for participating in this important effort, and good luck.

To the Teacher

Designed to sharpen reading and writing skills, this book, **New York State Coach, English Language Arts, Grade 6,** helps sixth-grade students prepare for the **New York State English Language Arts** exam New York State gives them each year.

This test does <u>not</u> test how many reading and writing details students have memorized. Instead, it tests how well they understand and execute some of the ideas and skills they need to be good readers and writers.

The three units of the **Coach** are each divided into chapters and lessons that align with New York State assessment standards. Using those standards as guides, each lesson begins with skills instruction, then provides examples for practicing those skills. The *Quick Coach* tools that follow each question help students answer the questions. Similarly, *Coached Reading* sections guide students through practice passages and questions, and *Test Practice* sections provide review and test-like questions that assess students' understanding and familiarizes them with the test's format.

Have your students work through the book carefully, and remind them that the concept, or "big idea," behind an answer is more important than the answer itself. There are no shortcuts to doing well on the **New York State English Language Arts test**.

To maximize the benefit of this book, first give your students the pretest in a setting that's as close to the actual test setting as possible. Then, use the answer key correlations and competencies analysis charts in the *Teacher's Guide* to identify where students need the most work.

When you're in class, take time to review each chapter and lesson with your students, and give them plenty of opportunities to ask questions. Also, review the *Thinking It Through* and *Example* questions. Make sure your students can not only provide the correct answers, but they can tell <u>why</u> those answers are correct.

Outside the classroom, instruct your students to read and study this book at home, and encourage parents to review the material with them as well. The more students practice, the better they're likely to do on the test.

As you know, teachers and parents working together can help the students succeed. Thank you for participating in this important effort. And good luck.

PRETEST

English
Language Arts
BOOK 1

Session 1

*D*irections
The following article describes the endangered lives of elephants in Africa. Read "Local Stampede Highlights Elephant Problem," by Constantine Miller. Then do Numbers 1 through 5.

LOCAL STAMPEDE HIGHLIGHTS ELEPHANT PROBLEM

by Constantine Miller, *staff writer*

SAHARA DESERT, AFRICA— Late yesterday afternoon, local residents reported what has become an unusual sight: a stampede of African elephants. While the elephants reportedly trampled some area gardens and knocked over chairs, residents reported being pleased with the event overall. They said they hoped it meant that the great creatures would return to the area.

"For so long, we've been losing these magnificent creatures to poachers," said area resident Bill Katasa. "These people have been hunting these great animals, and we've been losing them in great numbers. It's been so sad, really. So this stampede? It's actually a good problem to have. I'll take a few ruined plants!"

Targeted for Their Tusks

According to local researcher Mattie Reilly, yesterday's event does indeed mark a comeback of sorts for the African elephant. During the 1980s, she said, people hunted African elephants in great numbers. They wanted the animals for their ivory tusks. Some elephants, Reilly said, were at greater risk than others. "You see, depending on where they live, African elephants have long or short tusks," she said. "In crowded forests, elephants have short tusks. They can move more freely that way. In the more open, grassy savannah, however, elephants have very long, curved tusks. And that makes them more attractive to hunters."

12

"I guess a little part of me knows why the hunters do it. I empathize," Katasa said. "Ivory is highly valued around the world. It's used in jewelry, statues, piano keys, and many other things. Many people here are really, really poor. Hunting elephants is one of the few ways they have to make money and survive. So they just find the elephants irresistible. It's an unfortunate mix."

At Risk of Extinction

According to Reilly, poachers have killed countless elephants already. "Back in the early 1980s, when I was starting out in research, there were about 1 million of these beautiful animals," she said. "I was so excited to study these creatures, and I could do so pretty easily because there were so many. Back then, stampedes were a pretty regular thing."

Soon though, things began to change, Reilly said. "The hunters were really greedy. They were hunting too much. Each day, they killed over 270 elephants!"

As a result, Reilly said, by 1990 the number of elephants had dwindled to about 600,000. "We lost almost half our elephants before someone in this country decided to do something," she said. "Finally they did." According to Reilly, that "something" was a ban on ivory in 1989.

A Turning Point

"It's true," Katasa said. "People like me were outraged about losing so many precious elephants. But the good news is once people decided to act, they really decided to act." Katasa said that animal-protection organizations took steps to make people aware of the problem. In addition, some big companies helped by refusing to buy ivory. "The best companies even asked their customers to stop buying ivory," Katasa said. "And the best part is that many people did!"

Today, Reilly said that people have found a new, creative way to make money from elephants. Holding paintbrushes in their trunks, elephants make paintings. "If you can believe that!" Reilly said. These paintings are later sold to support elephant-conservation efforts. "It's a beautiful solution in many ways," Reilly said. "Not only do we get beautiful paintings from beautiful creatures, we get to keep those beautiful creatures around."

Go On

1 Read this sentence from the passage.

> **"I guess a little part of me knows why the hunters do it. I empathize."**

In this sentence, what does "empathize" mean?

A understand

B disagree

C investigate

D disapprove

2 Each of the following belongs in the "A Turning Point" section **EXCEPT**

F Many people have bought the paintings; hopefully they will continue to do so.

G A boycott like that would affect any business.

H Elephants tend to prefer to use a right or left tusk.

J Eventually, the sale of ivory was made illegal all around the world.

3 It is likely that the hunters prefer hunting savannah elephants because they

A are slower than the forest elephants

B have longer tusks and therefore more ivory

C have a better chance of making better paintings

D are easier to catch in the grassy open

4 It is likely that companies refused to buy ivory because

F they wanted to satisfy their customers

G they wanted to spend more time making paintings

H they wanted to reduce the demand for ivory

J they wanted to spend more money raising elephants

5 According to the article, why is ivory valued so highly?

A because there is so little of it

B because the tusks look nice

C because it is used to make jewelry

D because elephants are an endangered species

D*irections*
In "The New Vestments," a poem by Edward Lear, a man goes out walking in some extremely odd clothing. Read to see what happens, then do Numbers 6 through 10.

The New Vestments
by Edward Lear

There lived an old man in the Kingdom of Tess,
Who invented a purely original dress;
And when it was perfectly made and complete,
He opened the door, and walked into the street.
By way of a hat, he'd a loaf of Brown Bread,
In the middle of which he inserted his head;
His Shirt was made up of no end of dead Mice,
The warmth of whose skins was quite fluffy and nice;
His Drawers were of Rabbit-skins; so were his shoes;
His Stockings were skins—but it is not known whose;
His Waistcoat and Trousers were made up of Pork Chops;
His Buttons were Jujubes, and Chocolate Drops;
His coat was all Pancakes with jam for a border,
And a girdle of Biscuits to keep him in order;
And he wore all over, as a screen from bad weather,
A Cloak of green Cabbage-leaves stitched all together.
He had walked a short way, when he heard a great noise
Of all sorts of Beasticles, Birdlings, and Boys;
And from every long street and dark lane in town
Beasts, Birdies, and Boys in a tumult rushed down.
Two Cows and a half ate his Cabbage-leaf Cloak;

Go On

Four Apes seized his Girdle, which vanished like smoke;
Three Kids ate up half of his Pancaky Coat,
And the tails were devoured by an ancient He Goat;
An army of Dogs in a twinkling tore up his
Pork Waistcoat and Trousers to give to their Puppies;
And while they were growling, and mumbling the Chops,
Ten Boys snatched the Jujubes and Chocolate Drops.
He tried to run back to his house, but in vain,
For Scores of fat Pigs came again and again;
And now from the housetops with screechings descend,
Striped, spotted, white, black, and gray Cats without end,
They jumped on his shoulders and knocked off his hat,
When Crows, Ducks, and Hens made quick work of that,
They speedily flew at his sleeves in a trice,
And utterly tore up his Shirt of dead Mice;
And he said to himself as he bolted the door,
"I will not wear similar clothes anymore,
Anymore, anymore, anymore, nevermore!"

6 Which statement best expresses the theme of the poem?

   F   Be kind to animals.

   G   Use food in unusual ways.

   H   Eat all your vegetables.

   J   Learn from your mistakes.

7 Read this sentence from the passage.

"Beasts, Birdies, and Boys in a tumult rushed down."

In this sentence, what does "tumult" mean?

   A   long street

   B   loud rush

   C   calm group

   D   lush garden

8 It is likely that the author of this poem feels

   F   It's okay to try new things as long as you learn from them.

   G   People in kingdoms should be treated better than everyone else.

   H   Only certain kinds of people should wear certain kinds of things.

   J   It's okay to make fun of people who are different.

9 Which excerpt from the poem uses rhyme, a literary technique in which an author pairs two words that sound alike?

   A   "By way of a hat, he'd a loaf of Brown Bread,

      In the middle of which, he inserted his head"

   B   "When Crows, Ducks, and Hens made a mincemeat of that,

      They speedily flew at his sleeves in a trice"

   C   "Who invented a purely original dress;

      And when it was perfectly made and complete"

   D   "And utterly tore up his Shirt of dead Mice;

      They swallowed the last of his shirt with a squall"

10 Which of the following best describes the setting of this poem?

   F   in the kingdom's castle

   G   at a farm

   H   in the kingdom's streets

   J   at a festival

Go On

D irections

"They Both Saw the Light," by Ari Butler, describes the competition to create a functional light bulb. Read the following passage. Then do Numbers 11 through 15.

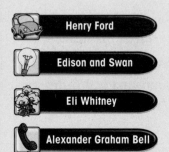

Henry Ford

Edison and Swan

Eli Whitney

Alexander Graham Bell

Alfred Nobel

They Both Saw the Light

by Ari Butler

Today they're considered common, everyday and everyplace. They're things we're used to; things we probably don't think much about. They're certainly not things we're used to doing without.

But there was a time, back in the 1870s, when things were different, very different. You see, back then, people didn't have the things we're now so used to, things like the common, everyday electric light. They had gas or oil lamps—good, old-fashioned flames.

On separate tracks, but at the same time, two men set on the path to discovering the electric light. The first was American-born Thomas Edison, a man who had learned and invented all his life. He was determined now to conquer the electric light. But there was a second man, an Englishman, with the same drive. His name was Joseph Swan. Like Edison, he too, was bent on conquering the electric light. Each wanted to be the first to create a light bulb that worked.

At the outset, it wasn't clear who would win the race. Both men were armed with considerable talent. Each alone had awe-inspiring intellect and drive.

In a light bulb, electricity flows through a thin strip of material. This material, called a filament, glows white-hot. And when it glows it creates light. The problem was not getting the filament to glow; it generally did that quite easily. The challenge was to get that filament to glow for longer than a few seconds.

Session 1

From their labs in different countries, Edison and Swan each experimented with different kinds of filaments. From paper to iron to hair, they tried every material they could think of. For a long time, though, nothing worked. Every material they tested either did not light, or it caught aflame and burned out after just a few seconds.

Needless to say, Edison and Swan were both perplexed. They had both accomplished so much, but this problem was proving formidable. Neither inventor, though, was willing to give up.

Fortunately, neither had to wait too much longer for success. At nearly the same time, both men hit on a solution. They both used a filament made of carbon. And that was the filament that finally worked. When it was lighted, it didn't just burn; it burned for several hours!

Both men may have made it through the race neck and neck, but Swan made it to the finish line faster. He registered the patent for the light bulb in 1878. One year later, Edison did the same. At the time Swan registered his patent, light bulbs only lasted about 150 hours. Today, they are good for about 1,850 more.

Edison may have failed to file his patent first, but he is clearly the better inventor. His original light bulb burned longer than Swan's. Swan's lasted for 150 hours, but Edison's burned for 1,200 just one year later. He was the first to bring electric light into people's homes. And that, say some, was really the biggest fight.

Go On

Session 1

11 Why was this invention so important?

A It was a better form of light than gas lamps or candles.

B All inventions are important, large or small.

C Because Thomas Edison was one of our greatest inventors.

D Because everyone wanted Swan to win the race to invent it.

12 According to the article, which of the following is true about light bulbs?

F They are one of the greatest inventions.

G Carbon filament burns the longest.

H Swan's bulb was less impressive than Edison's bulb.

J Swan was a better inventor than Edison.

13 All of the following were early materials used to make light bulb filaments **EXCEPT**

A iron

B paper

C hair

D gold

14 Which of the following is a way Edison and Swan were different?

F how talented they were

G what they filed patents for

H when they invented the light bulb

J where they came from

15 Read the following sentence from the passage.

They had both accomplished so much, but this problem was formidable.

In this sentence, what does the word "formidable" mean?

A invented

B tough

C easy

D talented

*D*irections

This is the story of a girl who faces up to a horrible monster—or does she? Read "To My Rescue," by Val Martin. Then do Numbers 16 through 20.

To My Rescue

by Val Martin

I know it didn't make a lot of sense to most people, not even to my dad. But I didn't care. I was scared. And that seemingly harmless little lake, that little pool just past our backyard? I didn't care how small it was—It just plain scared me.

It was Dad, after all, who always said, "It's not the quantity, it's the quality." Well, if quality counted, that lake was doing just fine. In fact, it was the head of the scary department. 'Cause it may have been small, but it was deep, and cold. Most of all, it was green, and slimy—very, very slimy. It was so green and slimy, you couldn't see the bottom!

Which, in a way, was just fine with me. I didn't really want to see what was down there. My older sister, Marcia, had me convinced a swamp monster lived there. I could only imagine what it looked like. Believe me, my imagination was racing constantly. And what was worse than thinking the monster was out there, just a few steps away? Marcia convinced me it was coming for me, and any other little girls nearby!

Go On 31

So each night in bed, I'd pull my covers over my eyes and try to pretend the swamp monster wasn't out there. But it was hot in the summers and without the window open, it would have been suffocating. I was so torn about that window: I wanted to let the air in, but I wanted more to keep the swamp monster away. That flimsy little screen didn't seem like nearly enough to keep the monster at bay.

On the nights I felt brave, and not too, too hot, I'd gather up the courage, leap out of bed, and slam the window shut. When I awoke, all sweaty and tousled, the window was always open—and I was always still alive. But though I'd survived another night, each morning like that I thought, "Next time I'll be gone, just a trail of swamp weeds behind me."

So the night it happened, I wasn't surprised. I'd been expecting something like this for a long, long time. "Hellllllllllllloooooooooooo!" came the first plaintive cry, just after nine. Then it happened again. "Hellllllllllloooooooooooooo!" again cried the voice. From beneath the covers in my bed, I began to shiver instantly. Then, more chillingly, I realized something. That must be the swamp monster! He'd finally come to get me! "This is perfect, just what I've always wanted," I thought to myself.

But in the next instant, though, I shed my fear. I had enough, I decided. The swamp monster and I would finally meet. Leaping up, I catapulted downstairs and toward the voice coming from just outside. In a burst of energy, I grasped the front door handle and flung the door open wide. Without hesitating, I flung myself down the stairs and toward the lake. But I got just two steps before I connected with somebody. A very big somebody. It was the worst that could have happened. I'd touched the swamp monster.

"Now, hold on there!" said the voice I'd heard before, though this time it sounded much kinder. Stepping back, I looked up slowly. My eyes met those of our delivery woman, Hallie. "What's the big hurry?" she asked with a smile. "I just need somebody to sign for this package. But it doesn't have to be so urgent, really."

The relief I felt was immediate and overwhelming. In that moment, I realized something that was, for me, pretty earth-shattering. I no longer had to worry about the swamp monster. I was free. Because I had faced him down. And I had survived.

Session 1

16 Why does Marcia want to scare her sister?

   F Marcia is scared herself.

   G Marcia believes in the swamp monster.

   H Marcia wants the lake to herself.

   J Marcia is just teasing her because she is younger.

17 This story is told from the

   A fourth person point of view

   B third person point of view

   C second person point of view

   D first person point of view

18 Why does the narrator say the lake is the "head of the scary department"?

   F She is easily frightened.

   G The lake is very pleasant.

   H The lake seems extremely frightening to her.

   J The lake is very deep.

19 The style and the wording of the story are meant to make readers feel

   A happy

   B nervous

   C bored

   D angry

20 The monster in this story represents

   F the narrator's swimming skills

   G the narrator's fear

   H the narrator's sister

   J the narrator's father

Go On

Directions

In this retelling of a Japanese folktale, a woman makes an interesting discovery when she puts on a special cap. Read "The Listening Cap," retold by Carmen Thompson. Then do Numbers 21 through 26.

The Listening Cap
by Carmen Thompson

There once lived a poor woman who visited the shrine of her guardian spirit every morning. She was so devoted that one day the guardian spirit left her a gift: a small, green cap.

Delighted, the woman immediately put on the cap. To her great surprise, she was able to understand what all the living creatures of the forest were saying—all the animals, all the trees, all the plants. "Why—It's a listening cap!" she cried.

Just then, two robins perched on a nearby branch. After a pause, they began to converse.

"It's so sad about the maple tree," said the one. "How true," replied the other, nodding. "I heard it crying again last night. Do you know the story behind the tree's sadness?" The woman leaned toward the birds slightly.

"Yes," the first robin said as the woman listened: "I was there the day it happened, in fact. The mayor chopped the maple down to make room for a teahouse in his garden. He destroyed that poor tree—except for its roots." The woman gasped, then quickly pressed her fingers to her mouth.

"Those roots are still there, though they're withering under the tea house," the bird continued. "That's why the tree still cries out in pain. Part of it is left, but it's dying, slowly and painfully. Imagine that: a once-vital tree with no sunshine, no food. It's in prison, dying, under the tea house." The woman looked as if she were about to cry.

"So is that why the mayor is so weak and sickly?" asked the second bird, wrinkling its brow. "Is this how the tree is paying him back?"

"It is indeed," the first bird replied. "The maple's put a dark spell on him. On the day it finally dies, the mayor will, too." At this, the woman again gasped. This time, she couldn't control herself.

In an instant, though, she knew just what to do. She rushed home and donned a costume. She found a white coat and a stethoscope. She would pose as a doctor.

In disguise, the woman approached the mayor's grand house. Gravely concerned about her spouse, the mayor's wife was thrilled to see a "doctor" when she opened the door. "Please, do come in!" the wife implored. "We've tried all the known remedies to make my husband well, but we're always willing to listen to somebody else."

Barely hesitating upon seeing the mayor, the woman asked, "So just when did your husband build that tea house of yours?"

"Why, just last year," the wife responded, looking puzzled.

"And your husband's been sick ever since?" the woman asked.

"Why, yes—I know you're a doctor, but how could you tell that?" "It's a special talent," the woman replied.

"There's one quick and easy remedy to what ails your husband," the woman continued. At this, the wife straightened and gave the woman her full attention. "If you want your husband to live, tear down the tea house at once. But more important, tend to the roots of the maple tree beneath it. If you help the tree grow strong again, your husband will grow strong again, too."

With that, the wife immediately beckoned her garden staff. Within hours, the tea house had been demolished. A few weeks after, with sunshine, watering, and the wife's tender care, the once-dying maple again began sending green shoots into the air. By then, the mayor had fully recovered, too. Just as the "doctor" had ordered and promised.

Go On

21 Which part of the story uses irony, the technique in which an author gives you significant information that a character does not have?

A The mayor recovers when the teahouse is destroyed.

B The mayor is very sick and his wife does not know what to do.

C The maple tree was cursed when the mayor built his teahouse.

D The tea house was destroyed to get rid of the curse.

22 Why does the wife agree to tear down the tea house?

F She cares about her husband and his health.

G She wants to get rid of the birds living there.

H She wants to make room near her main house.

J She is afraid the woman will hurt her husband.

23 According to the story, why is the maple tree crying?

A because it is lonely

B because no birds live in it

C because it was chopped down to make room for the teahouse

D because it does not like the mayor

24 What is probably the author's opinion about the mayor?

F He is a very brave man.

G He is a wise man.

H He is a foolish man.

J He is a good man.

25 It is likely that the woman in the passage

A wants to be a doctor

B needs help with listening

C cares deeply about nature

D wants to be mayor

26 This story is mainly about

F the death of a tree

G the magical powers of a listening cap

H the mayor's wife

J the talking birds

STOP

English Language Arts

BOOK 2

This test asks you to write about what you have listened to or read. Your writing will NOT be scored on your personal opinions. It WILL be scored on:

- how clearly you organize and express your ideas
- how accurately and completely you answer the questions
- how well you support your ideas with examples
- how interesting and enjoyable your writing is
- how correctly you use grammar, punctuation, and paragraphs

 Whenever you see this symbol, be sure to plan and check your writing.

Session 2

Session 2

Listening

*D*irections

In this part of the test, you will listen to the article, "Alexander, the Dwarf, and the Troll." Then you will answer some questions to show how well you understood what was read.

You will listen to the article twice. As you listen carefully, you may take notes on the articles anytime you wish during the readings. You may use these notes to answer the questions that follow. Use the space on Pages 30 and 31 for your notes.

This article is about a man and a dwarf who meet in the woods. It is adapted from a folktale that started in Denmark. Here are the spellings of some words that may be unfamiliar to you:

- meager
- porridge
- knarled

Go On

Notes

"Alexander, the Dwarf, and the Troll"

Session 2

Notes

"Alexander, the Dwarf, and the Troll"

STOP

27 In the box below, write how the problem in "Alexander, the Dwarf, and the Troll" is solved.

Problem	Solution
Alexander has to hide from the troll wife, so she will not eat him.	

28 How does the dwarf repay Alexander, and what is he repaying him for? Use details from the story to support your answer.

_____

_____

_____

_____

_____

_____

29 What kind of character is Alexander, and how does he differ from the troll wife? Use information from the story to support your answer.

_____

_____

_____

_____

_____

_____

Planning Page

You may PLAN your writing for Number 30 here if you wish, but do NOT write your final answer on this page. Your writing on this Planning Page will NOT count toward your final score. Write your final answer on Pages 34 and 35.

NOTICE: Photocopying any part of this book is forbidden by law.

Go On

33

Session 2

30 How might the story and its theme differ if Alexander had refused to help the dwarf? Use examples from the story to support your answer.

Be sure to include the:

- main events of the story you heard
- theme of the story you heard
- main events of the new story
- theme of the new story

 Check your writing for correct spelling, grammar, and punctuation.

_____

_____

_____

_____

_____

_____

_____

_____

_____

_____

_____

_____

_____

Session 2

STOP

35

English

Language Arts

BOOK 3

Session 3

Reading

Directions

In this part of the test, you are going to read a poem called "Pirate of Don Durk of Dowdee" and an article called "Captain Kidd—Some Kind of Pirate." You will answer questions and write about what you have read. You may look back at the articles as often as you like.

Pirate Don Durk of Dowdee

by Mildred Plew Meigs

Ho, for the Pirate Don Durk of Dowdee!
He was as wicked as wicked could be,
But oh, he was perfectly gorgeous to see!
The Pirate Don Durk of Dowdee.

His conscience, of course, was as black as a bat,
But he had a floppety plume on his hat
And when he went walking it jiggled—like that!
The plume of the Pirate Dowdee.

His coat it was handsome and cut with a slash,
And often as ever he twirled his mustache
Deep down in the ocean the mermaids went splash,
Because of Don Durk of Dowdee.

Moreover, Dowdee had a purple tattoo,
And struck in his belt where he buckled it through
Were a dagger, a dirk, and a squizzamaroo,
For fierce was the Pirate Dowdee.

So fearful he was he would shoot at a puff,
And always at sea when the weather grew rough
He drank from a bottle and wrote on his cuff,
Did Pirate Don Durk of Dowdee.

Oh, he had a cutlass that swung at his thigh
And he had a parrot called Pepperkin Pye,
And a zigzaggy scar at the end of his eye
Had Pirate Don Durk of Dowdee.
He kept in a cavern, this buccaneer bold,
A curious chest that was covered with mold,
And all of his pockets were jingly with gold!
Oh jing! went the gold of Dowdee.

31 How did the pirates live? Use details from "Pirate Don Durk of Dowdee" to support your answer.

_____

_____

_____

_____

_____

_____

Go On

Captain Kidd—
Some Kind of Pirate

By Naomi Walters

One thing's for sure: Captain Kidd was famous for being a pirate. His name is common in tales about pirates, but his career as a pirate didn't last very long.

Captain Kidd was born in Scotland in 1645, as William Kidd. He didn't start out as a pirate. In fact, he started out as the successful captain of a private ship. During those years, he often sailed to the Caribbean. Once he tired of those adventures, he moved to New York City in search of new excitement. Kidd wasn't willing to stay in one place for too long, though. In 1695, he left for England. His next goal was to secure a spot in the Royal Navy, but he didn't achieve that. Instead, he got a special license that he needed to capture French and pirate ships.

Kidd and his crew earned a lot of money, and things were going pretty smoothly for them until 1696. That year, Kidd and his crew left port in England. They were headed to New York City on the Adventure Galley. But no one, least of all Kidd, knew just what kind of adventure was in store.

Along the way, the British Navy stopped Kidd's ship and took much of his crew. When he reached New York City, Kidd had to hire many new men. Kidd was behind in his journey, and he was desperate. He promised his new crew 60 percent of the money he would earn, even though he'd already promised that money to the owners of the ship.

This crew didn't stand for Kidd's antics for very long. They grew tired of attacking only French and pirate ships, which were the only ships for which Kidd had a license. They decided to revolt. During the revolt, Kidd killed one of the crew members with a blow to the head. The rest of the crew then backed down, but the incident changed Kidd forever. Now, *whatever* ships came his way, he would attack. He was no longer a private, law-abiding captain. He was officially a pirate.

That was in 1697. A few successful ship attacks later, he captured the Quedah Merchant, a rich Indian ship loaded with silk, guns, spices, and gold. He sailed it to the Caribbean, where he learned that England wanted to arrest him for being a pirate. He went to Boston in 1700 to try to bribe his way out of his trouble, but the governor there arrested him and sent him to England. Just four short years after his pirate career began, Captain Kidd was hanged for piracy and murder. While his career may have been cut short, Kidd still became infamous.

Kidd was very good at keeping a secret. Before he died, he bragged that he had buried 40,000 British pounds of treasure somewhere. To date, only 10,000 pounds have ever been found.

Go On

32   Why did Captain Kidd become a pirate? Complete the chart below. Use examples from "Captain Kidd—Some Kind of Pirate" in your answer.

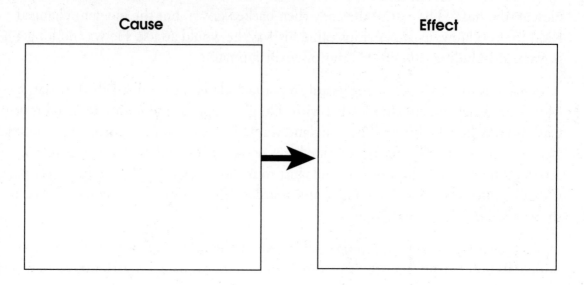

Cause   **Effect**

33   How did the lives of Pirate Don Durk and Captain Kidd compare? Use information from both passages to support your answer.

_____

_____

_____

_____

_____

Session 3

Planning Page

You may PLAN your writing for Number 34 here if you wish, but do NOT write your final answer on this page. Your writing on this Planning Page will NOT count toward your final score. Write your final answer on Pages 44 and 45.

NOTICE: Photocopying any part of this book is forbidden by law.

Go On 43

Session 3

34 Describe what a trip on one of Captain Kidd's ships might have been like. Use evidence from both passages to support your answer.

Be sure to include:

- the way the ship might look
- a description of crew members
- the kinds of adventures you might have
- as many details as possible

 Check your writing for correct spelling, grammar, and punctuation.

_____

_____

_____

_____

_____

_____

_____

_____

_____

_____

_____

_____

_____

_____

STOP

STOP

UNIT 1

Reading and Writing Fiction, Poetry, Drama and Other Forms

GETTING THE IDEA

In the world of literature, there's a lot to read and even more to entertain you. In this unit, you'll not only learn how to identify the different types of literature—poetry, fiction, drama, and nonfiction—you'll start to delve into the elements that make a story work.

In addition to plot, you'll learn about things like climax and foreshadowing. You'll learn more about what makes characters work, and how to write settings that help bring them to life. Theme is another thing you'll learn more about. And you can apply many themes to life, not just to the things you read.

You'll find reading's different once you've finished this unit. You'll better appreciate the colorful language and figures of speech that make words come right off the page.

Finally, you'll get the chance to write your own poems and stories. After all, literature is best enjoyed when experienced first-hand.

Standards: S2.I.1.A Read and view texts and performances from a wide range of authors, subjects, and genres.

S2.I.1.B Understand and identify the distinguishing features of the major genres and use them to aid their interpretation and discussion of literature.

CHAPTER 1

Part 1: Reading to Discover

Elements of Literature

Lesson 1: Telling the Genres Apart

You read many kinds of things—short stories, articles, poems, and books—so how do you tell those things apart? By their unique characteristics.

The table below describes four types of literature. How do the types compare?

	Definition	**Examples**
Fiction	Stories that use sentences and paragraphs to describe imaginary characters and events	Short stories Novels
Nonfiction	Stories that use sentences and paragraphs to describe real characters and events	Biographies Newspaper articles
Poetry	Writing in groups of lines called stanzas that uses expressive language, rhythm, and sometimes rhyme to communicate feelings	Nursery rhymes Song lyrics
Drama	Writing that is meant to be acted out using setting notes, stage directions, and dialogue	Plays Television scripts

When you look at this table, how do fiction and nonfiction compare? Fiction is made up while nonfiction is real, but both use sentences and paragraphs, or something called prose. Poetry, in contrast, does not use prose. Instead, it breaks sentences between lines and groups them into stanzas. It also uses rhythm and sometimes rhyme.

So where does drama fit in with all this? It's a little different from both poetry and prose. While it uses full sentences like prose and can be very expressive like poetry—drama is meant to be acted out—it includes things prose and poetry both lack like setting notes and dialogue.

48

THINKING IT THROUGH Read the passage below, and then answer the question that follows.

Once I saw a little bird
Come hop, hop, hop.
And I cried, "Little bird,
Will you stop, stop, stop?"

I was going to the window
To say, "How do you do?"
When he shook his little tail
And away he flew.

Which type of literature is this passage? Give at least one reason to support your answer.

_____

_____

_____

 HINT! Are the lines arranged in paragraphs or stanzas? Which type of literature uses rhythm and rhyme?

Example 1

In May 1883, the world welcomed its "Eighth Wonder," the Brooklyn Bridge. Never before had the world seen a bridge so long. It stretched nearly 1,600 feet across the East River of New York City to connect Brooklyn and Manhattan.

When it opened, the Brooklyn Bridge was one of the world's greatest achievements. At the time, iron supported most bridges. The Brooklyn Bridge was different; it hung from huge steel cables. Two large towers, sunk in the riverbed at either of the bridge, held the cables above the water. Each tower stood 275 feet tall.

The bridge was special in other ways, too. It held six lanes of traffic, and had a unique walkway that ran down its middle. Today it may no longer be the world's longest suspension bridge, but the Brooklyn Bridge still inspires wonder among New Yorkers.

1° **What kind of passage is this?**

A fiction

B nonfiction

C poetry

D drama

Consider the subject of the passage, and the way it uses and arranges sentences. Note that it lacks things like setting notes and dialogue.

Example 2

TITLE: A Ghost? Or a Joke?

CHARACTERS: Kavi, Jamar, Mrs. Lightbear

SETTING: A school classroom, about 3 PM

KAVI: *(jumping up and down excitedly, pointing to the back of the classroom):*
Look, look! Over there! Over there! It's a ghost, a ghost! A real, live ghost!

JAMAR: *(looking bored):*
Come on, Kavi, you're such a jokester! Don't you know that when you joke too much, nobody believes you?

KAVI: *(still excited):*
But I'm not joking! Look! It's over there! And look fast before it disappears!

MRS. LIGHTBEAR: *(looking midly amused):*
Come on, you two, let's get back to work. The only thing that's going to disappear is the two of you, once you get your assignment done!

---

2 **What kind of passage is this?**

A   fiction

B   nonfiction

C   poetry

D   drama

Discuss your answer with your teacher or class.

Standard: S2.I.1.C Identify significant literary elements (including metaphor, symbolism, foreshadowing, dialect, rhyme, meter, irony, climax) and use those elements to interpret the work.

Lesson 2
Plot/Foreshadowing/Climax

In the last lesson, you learned about different kinds of stories. **Plot** is what happens in a story. Most plots have four main parts. Each one is linked to the next, like this:

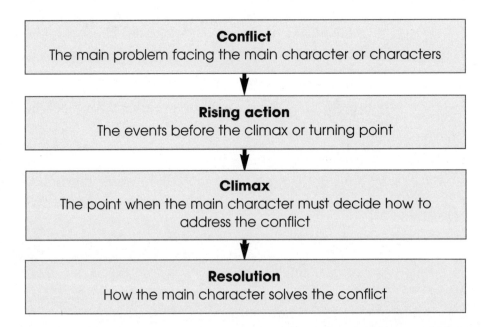

Conflict
The main problem facing the main character or characters

Rising action
The events before the climax or turning point

Climax
The point when the main character must decide how to address the conflict

Resolution
How the main character solves the conflict

For most stories, **conflict** is the most important part of the plot. This could be a problem a character has to solve. Or one character might want something another character wants, too. The events that grow out of the conflict, called **rising action**, reach a turning point. And then the story reaches its **climax**, usually the story's most exciting part. The main character must decide how to solve the conflict at the climax. Once that happens, **resolution** follows. Since the problem has been solved, the story ends.

Sometimes, you can tell when the parts of plot—like climax—are going to happen by a type of clue, or hint, called foreshadowing. Foreshadowing suggests what's going to happen, without being too obvious. The sky may darken to hint at trouble, for example.

Read the passage below, and then answer the question that follows.

Yoshe sat on her bed with no idea what to do. Looking back, she was amazed at how carefully she'd planned everything, except this moment. She'd trained hard to make the track team. She'd even gotten Mrs. Lightbear's recommendation. But her family wanted her to be an artist. Should she defy her parents? Or turn down her track spot and forget her dreams?

"I'm just not sure I can disappoint my parents," Yoshe thought to herself sadly. Just then, Yoshe's doorknob turned. Her stomach dropped, as her father entered.

"You know," said Yoshe's father softly, "I spoke with Mrs. Lightbear today. Is there something you'd like to tell me?"

Lowering her eyes, Yoshe paused. "Yes, Dad, there is."

"Wait," said her father, holding up his hand. "You know what? You don't have to," he said. "Follow your dream, Yoshe."

"So you mean I can be on the track team?" Yoshe exclaimed.

"Yes, Yoshe," replied her father. "That's exactly what I mean."

Where is the foreshadowing in this story? What does it hint at?

_____

_____

_____

_____

_____

 How does Yoshe feel about confronting her problem? How do you know that? What is the climax of this story?

Example 1

This is a Mexican folktale. Though Rabbit ran very fast, once, long ago, he'd challenged Tortoise to a race, and lost. Despite that, Rabbit liked to brag. Tired of such boasting, Frog challenged Rabbit to a race.

Rabbit was so confident he'd win, he let Frog choose the course. Frog chose a path through the tall swamp to the river, but first, he called all the frogs his size together. Frog lined up the frogs throughout the swamp—nearly 400 altogether—each about one good leap from the next. Only then did Frog direct Rabbit to start the race. "Finally!" Rabbit cried. "Now I'll prove once and for all that I'm the fastest creature!" In reply, Frog only smirked.

With a crowd gathered, Frog and Rabbit lined up side by side. With one drop of a flag, they were off—Rabbit like a shot! He ran for a long time before looking back for Frog. To Rabbit's surprise, Frog was right there beside him, leaping along! He didn't realize that it wasn't Frog at all. It was one of the many frogs lined up along the swamp.

With that, Rabbit doubled his resolve. He pinned back his ears and ran faster than ever. But try as he might, Rabbit couldn't seem to get ahead of Frog. As the finish line at the river loomed, Frog leaped ahead of Rabbit. As he did, he shouted, "You're too slow! I'm the fastest!"

Running too fast to make a quick stop, Rabbit landed with a loud splash in the river. Barely able to drag himself ashore, Rabbit lay on the bank, soggy and out of breath. It was a long time before anyone heard Rabbit boast about his running again.

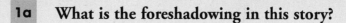

1a   **What is the foreshadowing in this story?**

A   Rabbit landed in the river.

B   Frog smirked before the race.

C   Rabbit lost a race to tortoise.

D   Frog lined up the other frogs.

Think about why Frog smirks before the race. Does it hint at something?

1b   **Read this sentence from the passage again.**

"As the finish line at the river loomed, Frog leaped ahead of Rabbit."

This sentence comes from which part of the plot?

F   conflict

G   rising action

H   climax

J   resolution

Discuss your answer with your teacher or class.

Standards: S2.I.1.A Read and view texts and performances from a wide range of authors, subjects, and genres.

S2.I.1.B Understand and identify the distinguishing features of the major genres and use them to aid their interpretation and discussion of literature.

S2.I.1.C Identify significant literary elements (including metaphor, symbolism, foreshadowing, dialect, rhyme, meter, irony, climax) and use those elements to interpret the work.

Coached Reading

> **The following passage is about a girl named Mary who secretly helped deliver letters written home by men in the Continental Army. As you read the passage, use the statements and questions in the margin to help your understanding.**

Your teacher may read this selection to you.

Black-Eyed Rebel

By Will Carleton

A boy drove to the city, his wagon loaded down
With food to feed the people of the British-governed town;
And the little black-eyed rebel, so innocent and sly,
Was watching for his coming from the corner of her eye . . .

He drove up to the market, he waited in the line;
His apples and potatoes were so fresh and fair and fine;
But long and long he waited, and no one came to buy,
Save the black-eyed rebel, watching from the corner of her eye.

"Now who will buy my apples?" he shouted, long and loud;
And "Who wants my potatoes?" he repeated to the crowd;
But from all the people 'round him came no word of reply,
Save the black-eyed rebel, answering from the corner of her eye.

What do you notice about the sentences of this passage?

How are these lines arranged? What are these groups called?

Do you notice anything about the words that end each line? Circle the words that seem the same.

For she knew that 'neath the lining of the coat he wore that day,
Were long letters from the husbands and the fathers far away,
Who were fighting for the freedom that they meant to gain or die;
And a tear like silver glistened in the corner of her eye.
But the treasures—how to get them? crept the questions through her mind,
Since keen enemies were watching for what prizes they might find;
And she paused a while and pondered, with a pretty little sigh;
Then resolve crept through her features, and a shrewdness fired her eye.

So she resolutely walked up to the wagon old and red;
"May I have a dozen apples for a kiss?" she sweetly said;
And the brown face flushed to scarlet; for the boy was somewhat shy,
And he saw her laughing at him from the corner of her eye . . .

Clinging 'round his brawny neck, she clasped her fingers white and small,
And then whispered, "Quick! The letters! Thrust them underneath my shawl!
Carry back again this package, and be sure that you are spry!"
And she sweetly smiled upon him from the corner of her eye. . . .

With the news of loved ones absent to the dear friends they would greet,
Searching for them who hungered for them, swift she glided through the street.
"There is nothing worth the doing that it does not pay to try,"
Thought the little black-eyed rebel, with a twinkle in her eye.

Which part of the plot unfolds in this part of the passage? Does the author give you a hint of what is to come?

Which part of the plot occurs here? Does another part of the plot occur here as well?

As you hear these words or speak them aloud, do you notice any kind of pattern? Which type of literature uses patterns like this?

Reread the passage, and ask yourself the questions in the margin again. Then do Numbers 1 through 6.

1 This passage could be described as an example of

   A fiction

   B nonfiction

   C poetry

   D drama

2 The climax of the passage occurs when

   F the boy drives into the city

   G Mary decides to hug the boy

   H the boy sells his potatoes to Mary

   J Mary buys the boy's apples

3 When do you know Mary has found a way to solve her conflict? What is this an example of? Write your answer on the lines below.

_____

_____

_____

_____

_____

_____

4 **The rising action of the passage occurs when**

A   Mary considers how to get the letters

B   Mary leaves with the letters

C   the boy hugs Mary in return for apples

D   the boy takes Mary's package

5 **What is the conflict in this passage?**

F   Mary must find a way to give the package to the boy.

G   The boy must sell all his produce before returning home.

H   The boy must get Mary's package to the soldiers in secret.

J   Mary must find a secret way to get the letters from the boy.

6 **How does Mary solve her conflict? When she does, which part of the plot occurs? Write your answer on the lines below.**

_____

_____

_____

_____

_____

Discuss your answer with your teacher or class.

Test Practice

> **Read the following passage about a girl in a movie theater. Then do Numbers 1 through 4.**

Drama On and Off the Screen

A s the music rose, the theater grew dark and silent. Even the teenagers in the back stopped chattering. As the coming attraction came on the screen, Gisele slouched into her seat and snickered. To her right she had her dinner, smuggled in from Paolo's Pizza Paradise.

Glancing around for the green jackets of Royal Cinema 14 staff, Gisele reached slowly for her secret paper bag. Ever so quietly, she reached inside the bag and withdrew her treasure. The sausage calzone she removed was truly paradise. The tomatoes, the spices, the sausage, the cheese. . . .

She was so absorbed in eating that she didn't notice anything around her, not even the first tap on her shoulder. The second tap was stronger and got her attention. Calmly, Gisele covered her calzone with a napkin and turned toward the tapping.

"You know you're not supposed to bring food in from outside," the boy said sternly.

"What food?" Gisele asked innocently.

"You don't fool me—I can smell it," the boy returned. I'm going to have to confiscate your calzone."

"What?" Gisele cried out.

"You can't do that!"

"Yes, I can," the boy said. "In fact, I have to."

Now, for the first time, Giesele started to worry. "But I'm starving!" she cried.

"You know at the concession stand we sell hot dogs, popcorn, nachos, candy," the boy offered. "You can easily buy something there."

Suddenly, an idea took root in Gisele's head. "Look," she said. "How 'bout you take my dessert, and we call it a deal. It's really good—a cannoli. And chocolate chip—my favorite." At this, the boy looked interested but conflicted. Gisele pressed on. "I've learned my lesson," she said. "I won't do it again. I'll lose my cannoli as punishment. Believe me, that's punishment enough."

"Very well," agreed the boy. "It's a deal—I'll take it."

Barely looking at the cannoli, the boy stepped outside the theater and dropped it into the nearest trash can. Back inside, Gisele again snuggled into her seat, relief washing over her face.

---

1 This passage reaches its climax when

A Gisele smuggles her dinner into the theater

B the boy throws out the cannoli

C Gisele gets the idea to offer the boy her cannoli

D the boy threatens to take Gisele's dinner

2 Read the following sentences from the passage.

" 'Very well,' agreed the boy. 'It's a deal—I'll take it.' "

What is this an example of?

F conflict

G rising action

H climax

J resolution

3 Which of the following is an example of foreshadowing?

A The boy deciding whether to take Gisele's cannoli

B Gisele snickering deviously as she settled in for dinner

C The boy threatening to take Gisele's dinner

D Gisele becoming too absorbed in dinner to notice the boy

4   What kind of passage is this? Give two or three examples to support your response.

_____

_____

_____

_____

_____

_____

_____

_____

_____

_____

_____

_____

_____

_____

_____

_____

_____

_____

_____

_____

_____

Read the following passage, which is adapted from a Native American folktale. Then do Numbers 5 through 8.

Coyote Brings Back Spring

Long ago, winter snows covered northern New York for 10 long months each year. While the short summer lasted, the Iroquois would gather food, but it was never enough to last the winter.

The people were hungry in their longhouses, and Coyote was hungry, too. The most clever of animals, he decided to bring back spring so the warmth could bring back food. Just one person threatened his plan: Old Woman, keeper of the seasons. She liked winter. For most of the year, she let it rule.

Coyote gathered the Iroquois people. "I'm going north to return spring to you," Coyote declared. Instantly, Quiet One, Strong Arm, and Sharp Knives stepped forward. "We'll help you," they replied together. Coyote couldn't help himself—he grinned widely. Already, he could feel his heart lifting.

Together, the little group marched northward toward Old Woman's home. Finally spying her lodge perched atop a steep, rocky hill, Coyote motioned to the group to be still. "Okay," Coyote addressed the group. "Let's do it now."

With that, Quiet One slipped into the lodge. Pretending to warm his hands over Old Woman's crackling fire, he melted some tree sap in his palms and began to befriend Old Woman. Before long, the two were chatting like old friends. "So just where do you keep spring?" Quiet One whispered sneakily after some time had passed.

"I haven't seen it in a while." No sooner had Old Woman pointed to a small bag under her table than Quiet One sprang forward and forced the warm sap into the woman's mouth. Her mouth was bound. Old Woman could not cry out.

Seizing the opportunity, Quiet One tossed the bag of spring outside. Strong Arm, in turn, threw it to the bottom of the hill. Old Woman could not cry out, but she could run. She chased the bag down the slope, but Sharp Knives was already waiting there, ready to act. Moments before Old Woman came to rest at his feet, he sliced the bag, setting the warm spring winds loose.

As a bright sun appeared and chased away the gray winter clouds, Coyote smiled again, this time more broadly.

5 What is the problem, or conflict, of this passage?

F The Iroquois want spring, and Old Woman wants winter.

G Quiet One wants to melt the tree sap, and Coyote wants him to leave the tree alone.

H Old Woman wants to get spring back, and the Iroquois want winter.

J The Iroquois people want food, but they have to fight Old Woman for it.

6 The reader gets a hint that Coyote feels better about his plan when he

A gathers the Iroquois people

B flashes his sharp teeth

C feels his heart lift

D sees Old Woman's lodge

7 This passage could best be described as an example of

F fiction

G nonfiction

H poetry

J drama

8 Where in the passage does the climax occur?

_____

_____

_____

Lesson 3
Character/Dialect

Characters are the people who make a story happen. Of course, sometimes they aren't people. They may be animals, or even objects! Most stories have at least one character, often more.

Especially in fiction stories, it's important that characters seem real. Why? So readers care about them. Authors can make characters seem real in different ways. Sometimes, a character may act or look a certain way that stands out. Sometimes, just one detail will help you remember a character. In most good stories, the characters will remind you of someone you know. Some characters may remind you of yourself.

NOTICE: Photocopying any part of this book is forbidden by law.

65

Read the passage below, and then answer the question that follows.

While the rest of her class chatted, Martine sat at her desk. A slight frown was creasing her forehead. Without knowing it, she squinted and began to rub her temple.

"I have to ace this test, too," Martine thought to herself as she tapped her pencil. Suddenly, she felt another tap on her shoulder. Martine turned to find Mrs. Lightbear smiling at her. Automatically, Martine smiled, too.

"Why such a serious look, Martine?" Mrs. Lightbear asked, peering over the girl's shoulder. "If I didn't know better, I would have thought you were studying science!"

Martine laughed. "Believe me, Mrs. Lightbear, I wish I was!"

What kind of person is Martine? How can you tell?

_____

_____

_____

 HINT! Think about what Martine says and how she acts. What kind of person does she seem like?

Speech, or dialogue, is one way authors bring characters to life. The words characters use and the way they say them can tell you a lot. Very proper grammar may suggest that a character has had a lot of education. Sometimes the way a character talks can tell you he is tough, or easily scared. Some characters may speak in dialect, which describes a way of talking that groups of people pick up. The key is: listen as you read.

Example 1

"But I don't want to go," Jamar protested, kicking the piano bench. "I'm not going!" The look of shock on his father's face momentarily stopped him, but Jamar pressed on.

"Come on, Dad, don't make me go," he tried again, his voice rising. "You know I'd rather stay here and practice the piano."

"Son," his father replied sternly in measured tones, "we have spoken about this before. My response to you remains firm: This is your sister's final basketball game. You promised earlier you would attend it with us. There will be no further discussion of this matter."

"Okay, Dad," Jamar said. "You're right, I'll go. And I'm sorry. I shouldn't have argued."

1a **From his speech, you can tell that Jamar's father is MOST LIKELY a**

A   soft-spoken person

B   very intelligent person

C   friendly person

D   silly person

Words like "wanna" and "gonna" suggest that Jamar is young.

1b **Which word BEST describes how Jamar feels when he shocks his father?**

F   shy

G   angry

H   confused

J   guilty

Jamar regrets arguing with his father.

Example 2

Yoshe was so nervous, she could barely get the words of her report out. The longer she stood at her desk, the more uncomfortable she grew. She just wanted this to be over. How much longer would she have to report on the zoo? Finally, she reached the part about the chimps. That meant she was nearly done. Just then, the class burst out laughing again. Could there be someone behind her? Yoshe turned. There was Kavi, hunched over, dangling his hands, pretending to be a chimp. Immediately, Yoshe turned bright red. Kavi, though, simply took a bow.

2 **How do Kavi and Yoshe compare as characters? Use two or three examples.**

_____

_____

_____

_____

_____

_____

_____

_____

SELF Coach Discuss your answer with your teacher or class.

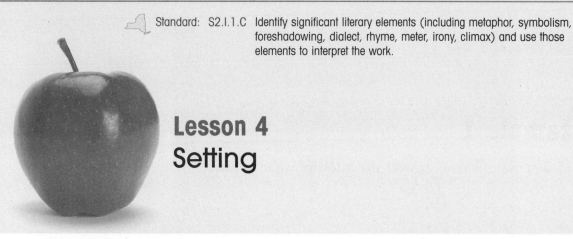

Lesson 4
Setting

Just like every story should have characters, every story should have a setting. The **setting** is the time and place in which a story occurs.

Sometimes, a setting is general, and you can figure it out using clues in the text. For example, a story that mentions trees, rocks, and deer probably takes place in a forest. At other times, though, the setting is stated directly. For example, a story could begin, "Spring in Cooperstown was the most beautiful time of year." Can you guess what the setting of the story below might be?

> Helen wriggled her toes in the sand, letting the hot sun beat on her face. Nearby, under a brightly colored umbrella, her aunt enjoyed the shade. As she sat under the crystal blue sky, Helen thought about swimming that day and tasting the warm, salty water on her lips. In just a few hours, she'd be back home, in the snow and cold. Once she got there, she'd e-mail her friends about all her adventures.

This passage doesn't specifically tell you the setting, but you can figure it out using the clues the narrator gives you. For example, Helen is in a warm, sandy place near water. This tells you she's probably on a beach. She also mentions e-mailing her friends upon returning home. e-mail is a technology people use today, so you can tell that the passage probably takes place in modern times.

Example 1

Read this passage, and answer the question that follows.

In 1678, Niagara Falls wasn't a famous place yet. The falls still hadn't really been explored by Europeans. Then Father Louis arrived. He'd left France determined to see and describe Niagara Falls that year. Why? He wanted the whole world to appreciate this great sight.

Father Louis was the first person to describe the falls fully. He was stunned by the falls' massive size. About 12,300 years before, at the end of the Ice Age, the falls first took shape. Huge amounts of melting ice released water into the Niagara River, and the great waterfall was born.

---

1 **What is the setting of this passage?**

A France in 1678

B Niagara Falls in 1678

C Niagara Falls in the Ice Age

D France in the Ice Age

Think about when Father Louis made his trip, and to where. Don't be confused by the passage's supporting details.

You've seen that fiction has a setting. Plays have settings as well. In drama, the **stage directions** tell the setting. They also tell the actors what to do before, during, and after they speak.

Example 2

Martine sits in the bleachers, twisting the hem of her dress in her fingers. She lets her eyes float over the disco balls and streamers, and over her classmates' faces below her. As the room darkens and the music grows louder, Ted approaches from under the farther basketball hoop, looking anxious.

TED: Um, hey, Martine. How's it going?

MARTINE: Oh, it's going okay, Ted. Not much going on, really, because. . .

The thump-thump-thump of the music drowns out Martine's last words. Ted strains visibly to hear what she says as he climbs the bleachers. Suddenly, Martine spots Jesse on the dance floor.

TED: I'm sorry, I couldn't hear what you said. But if you're not doing anything, I thought we could dance to this song.

MARTINE: I gotta go, Ted. Jesse promised to dance with me, and there he is.

Looking dejected as Martine climbs down the bleachers, Ted sits by himself.

2 **Where does this play take place?**

A   a cruise ship

B   a shopping mall

C   a school gym

D   a house

Discuss your answer with your teacher or class.

Standard: S2.I.1.C Identify significant literary elements (including metaphor, symbolism, foreshadowing, dialect, rhyme, meter, irony, climax) and use those elements to interpret the work.

Lesson 5
Theme

The **theme** of a story or poem is the idea or insight the author wants you to understand. Common themes include things like "One good turn deserves another," and "Slow and steady wins the race." A story may have one theme, or it may have several. Usually, the theme can be stated in a sentence.

So how can you tell a story's theme? The author generally won't tell you. You've got to figure it out. But that doesn't have to be hard. Imagine that you're the story's main character. What lesson should you have learned? What topics or issues kept coming up?

 Read the passage below, and then answer the question that follows.

   Louisa felt her heart beating as she eyed the pile of money before her. She had never expected to find something like this while digging in the back yard. Who would have thought something like this could happen—and to her? For a split second, Louisa considered keeping the bag of money her little secret. But it was only for a second. She knew the right thing to do, and she would do it. "Mom!" she called excitedly. "Guess what I found! We've got to tell someone!"

What is the theme of this story?

_____

_____

_____

 HINT! Think about what Louisa's actions in this passage mean.

Example 1

There was once a crow so thirsty he could barely caw. Then he saw a pitcher sitting on the ground. Hoping the vessel contained water, the crow plunged his beak into its opening. Sadly, there was just a little water at the bottom. There was not nearly enough water for the crow to reach.

Now feeling even more thirsty, the crow leaned back and thought for a moment. He couldn't give up. There had to be a way to get the water.

Gathering some strength, he plunged his beak into the pitcher again. Over and over again he strained to reach the water. He tilted the pitcher. He wedged his beak inside. Nothing seemed to work, though.

Still not willing to give up, the crow tried to break the pitcher. Then he tried to overturn it. He simply was not strong enough. Just as he was about to give up, he had one final thought.

With one last push, the crow leaned over, grasped a pebble in his beak, and dropped the pebble inside the pitcher. Over and over and over again the crow repeated his task. One by one, the pebbles filled the pitcher. Slowly, with each pebble, the water rose in the pitcher. Finally, after the crow dropped countless pebbles into the pitcher, the water reached the brim.

Perching himself on the pitcher's handle, the crow drank until he wasn't thirsty any more.

1 **What is the theme of this story?**

- **A** Be satisfied with what you've got.
- **B** Persistence is the key to success.
- **C** Know your limitations.
- **D** Appearances are often deceiving.

QUICK
Coach™

Think about why the crow was able, finally, to get the water.

Example 2

Waiting for the elevator with her class, Yoshe's knees trembled. The more she thought about the trip, the more nervous she got. She was afraid of heights, and the top of the Empire State Building was definitely high.

So far, Yoshe had managed her fear. When places were too high, she simply avoided them. This time was different, though. She had to conquer her fear. She couldn't avoid high places forever, after all. If she could just get on the elevator, she knew she'd be all right.

Last week, Yoshe had confided her fear in Mrs. Lightbear. Her teacher would help her, if she needed it. But Yoshe didn't have time for another thought. Just then, the light for the elevator turned green, and her classmates rushed by, scrambling for good spots in the car. Yoshe, though, stood rooted to the floor. Mrs. Lightbear asked gently, "You all right, Yoshe? Shall you and I wait here?"

Suddenly, Yoshe felt a surge. No, she certainly wasn't going to wait. Without pausing a moment more, Yoshe boarded the elevator. Then she shook her head, smiled, and breathed a huge sigh of relief. As Mrs. Lightbear took her place beside Yoshe, she leaned down and whispered quietly, "I'm really proud of you, because that was really brave."

2b **How does this theme compare with the theme in the last example? How are the stories the same or different?**

_____

_____

_____

_____

_____

2a **What is the theme of this story?**

A   It's best to face your fears.

B   Turn the other cheek.

C   Find a job you like.

D   Go with your strengths.

SELF Coach

Discuss your answer with your teacher or class.

Coached Reading

The following passage is about a father and son on a Greek island. As you read the passage, use the statements and questions in the margin to help your understanding.

 Your teacher may read this selection to you.

Daedalus and Icarus

Adapted from the original myth

Daedalus was an inventor from Athens who had gone to Crete to work at the court of King Minos. When Minos's wife, Queen Pasiphae, gave birth to a monster called the Minotaur, a ferocious combination of man and bull, King Minos asked Daedalus to build a labyrinth. The labyrinth was a gigantic, mind-twisting maze of walls from which no one could escape. There the Minotaur remained imprisoned, fed by young Athenian men whom the king sent to their deaths. King Minos kept the brutal creature alive but contained. The Minotaur was a weapon he could use to intimidate his enemies.

> What can you tell about King Minos? What kind of character is he so far?

One year, Theseus came to Crete to try to slay the Minotaur. Minos and Pasiphae's daughter, the princess Ariadne, fell in love with Theseus. Theseus and Ariadne begged Daedalus to help him kill the Minotaur and escape the labyrinth. Daedalus gave Ariadne a long, flaxen thread for Theseus to tie to the door of the labyrinth as he entered. Then, after killing the monster, he could find his way back out. It worked. Theseus killed the Minotaur and fled Crete with Ariadne.

> What character traits does Daedalus have? What can you tell about the setting?

King Minos was furious at having lost his daughter. He assumed no one could have killed the Minotaur and escaped without the help of Daedalus. So he seized the inventor and his son, Icarus, and shut them in the labyrinth. Daedalus knew he must gather all his mental energy to escape. He decided to build wings for himself and Icarus. The labyrinth was open to the sky, though the walls were too high to climb. But there were fruit and olives trees, and with these they managed to keep themselves alive. Daedalus painstakingly constructed wings from bird feathers he collected and wax he gathered from beehives.

At last, the wings were ready. Daedalus and Icarus waited for a windy day, and then they carried the wings to a long straightaway where they could get a running start. Daedalus helped Icarus into his wings, and as he did so, he reminded him, "These wings are made of wax. We cannot fly too close to the sun, or the wax will melt and the wings will fall apart."

Icarus was impatient to get started. "Yes, yes," he said, "I remember."

Daedalus kissed his forehead and donned his wings, and they started their run. A big gust of wind caught the underside of their wings as they ran. The father and son rose above the walls of the labyrinth. They were flying! They soared over the sea, escaping the island of Crete and the land of King Minos. Daedalus was relieved his invention had worked and they had escaped. But Icarus was enjoying his wings so much that he didn't hear his father calling to him. And he didn't notice that he was getting dangerously close to the hot sun.

All at once, the wax holding his wings together melted, the feathers flew apart, and Icarus plunged into the sea. Daedalus looked down to see feathers floating in the waves and was filled with grief and guilt. His two greatest inventions had caused the imprisonment and then the death of his beloved child. He buried his son on an island he named Icaria, and the sea into which Icarus fell came to be called the Icarian Sea.

What more does the reader learn here about the setting?

What clues does the reader get here about Icarus? How might these clues affect the theme?

How do the characters of Daedalus and Icarus compare? How does the setting impact the story?

What does the theme of this passage appear to be?

Reread the passage, and ask yourself the questions in the margin again. Then do Numbers 1 through 6.

1 Where does the beginning of this passage take place?

A in the sun

B in the labyrinth

C in Icarus's room

D in Crete

2 The reader can tell that King Minos is

F kind and caring

G intimidating but kind

H mean and intimidating

J polite but funny

3 How would the main idea of the passage be different if Icarus took Daedalus seriously? Write your answer on the lines below.

_____

_____

_____

_____

_____

NOTICE: Photocopying any part of this book is forbidden by law.

77

4 The reader can tell that the labyrinth is

A open at the top

B lacking windows

C lacking doors

D open at the sides

5 What is the theme of this passage?

F Don't believe what your family tells you.

G Disobey your elders when you want.

H Listen only to advice you like.

J Make sure to heed good advice.

6 How does Icarus relate to his father, Daedalus? Write your answer on the lines below.

_____

_____

_____

_____

_____

Discuss your answer with your teacher or class.

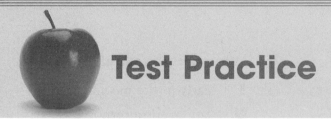

Test Practice

Read the following passage about a man and a bear. Then do Numbers 1 through 3.

Friends in Strange Places

As the sun crept over the horizon, an old man headed out to fish on a nearby lake. He hadn't been at it very long when he grew frustrated and gave up. "Maybe I'll feel better—and do better—after a little breakfast," the man thought as he headed back to his shack. "Maybe, when I come back, the fish'll be hungry, too."

Arriving home, the man immediately noticed something suspicious. His front door was open. Someone, or something, was inside. The man could feel his heart pounding as he crept to the side window. Peering inside, he was astonished to see a black bear opening his molasses jar . . . with his mouth! As the man watched, the creature pulled out the jar's cork, then threw back his head and took several long gulps. Molasses dripped down the bear's mouth and all over his paws.

The man could not contain his anger. He shouted through the window for the bear to leave. Startled, the bear bolted out the door, heading for the lake. As he ran, he waved his molasses-covered paws. Those paws attracted flies, mosquitoes, and all sorts of other bugs. It wasn't long before all those bugs became stuck to the bear!

Intent on avoiding the man, and loosening the bugs, the bear waded right in when he reached the lake. As he did, a trout jumped up to get the flies. Swatting instinctively, the bear sent the fish flying to shore. He did the same when another fish jumped . . . then another and another. Soon, the bear had collected a large pile of fish.

The old man, who had followed the bear, watched with amazement as the bear wandered to shore to sample the fish. The bear lined up a few of the fish, turned to the old man, and waved his now clean paw.

Stunned, the old man approached the shore. There he found the bear had left him nearly a dozen fish! Grateful, the man shouted his thanks to the bear. And from that day on, he never hunted bears again.

1 The word that **BEST** describes the man is

A   angry

B   uncaring

C   independent

D   unappreciative

2 When does this story take place?

F   early in the morning

G   late in the afternoon

H   after dinnertime

J   in the middle of the night

3 What is the theme of this passage? How would you change the passage to make its theme "Don't count your chickens before they're hatched"? Use specific examples.

_____

_____

_____

_____

_____

_____

_____

_____

_____

_____

_____

_____

_____

_____

Read the following passage about two lumberjacks. Then do Numbers 4 through 6.

Three Axes for Two Men

A lumberjack was trying to cut a particularly tough log. Determined to chop it, the man swung back powerfully . . . and accidentally tossed his axe deep into the nearby lake. The lumberjack stared sadly into the water. Just then, a nymph appeared.

Upon hearing the man's tale, she replied, "Don't worry. I'll get your axe."

With that, she dove into the water and came back up with a golden axe. The man explained it wasn't his, and she dove again. This time she returned with a silver one.

Again, the man said, "Not mine." So the nymph dove again, this time returning with the lost axe. The man claimed it, and she let him keep all three.

Overjoyed, the man crowed to his coworkers beneath the trees. One man listened intently, then immediately headed to the lake and tossed in his axe on purpose. Again the nymph appeared. When the man told her he'd lost his axe, she dove as before. Again she pulled up a golden axe on the first try.

"Is this your axe?" she asked.

"Yes! It is!" the man cried, reaching for the prize.

"But it's not," she replied, keeping the axe out of his reach. "And for what you've done, you'll have no axe!" With that, she disappeared.

4 Where does this passage take place?

A   in a wood store

B   in the lumberjack's home

C   in the nymph's home

D   in the woods

5 The theme of this passage is

F   Honesty is the best policy.

G   Be friends with everyone.

H   Work hard and play hard.

J   Trust those who give you things.

6 What is the best way to describe the first lumberjack? Compare him to the second one.

_____

_____

_____

_____

_____

_____

CHAPTER

Literary Techniques

Lesson 6: Metaphor and Simile

When you're writing, picking the right word helps express your meaning. But what if the right word just isn't there? Or what if you'd like to say it in an original way? Authors often use figures of speech to express meaning imaginatively. The most common figures of speech are metaphors and similes.

Metaphors

A **metaphor** compares two different things without using "like" or "as." A metaphor often uses a version of the verb "to be" (like "is"). A metaphor is an implied comparison, which means it relates two items but lets the reader determine just how they compare. The language isn't literal. Consider the following example:

> Kavi and Jamar loved the puppet show. They were laughing, clapping, and singing along. Try as they might, though, the boys just could not get Martine to join in. When Martine finally wandered away, Jamar poked his elbow into Kavi's side and said, "Martine is a stick in the mud."

What exactly does Jamar mean? Does he mean that Martine is literally a piece of wood in mud? No. He is suggesting that Martine is boring. Martine probably joins in at some point, just not all the time. This exaggeration, though, helps us see Martine as someone who isn't much fun.

Read the passage below, and then answer the question that follows.

The young parents feathered their nest before the baby arrived.

What makes this sentence a metaphor?

_____

_____

_____

HINT! Without using the words "like" or "as," metaphors compare two unlike things to imply something.

Example 1

1 **Read the following sentence.**

Mrs. Lightbear is a walking encyclopedia.

The meaning of this statement is closest to which of the following?

A Mrs. Lightbear is a lot of fun.

B Mrs. Lightbear is my favorite teacher.

C Mrs. Lightbear is quite shy.

D Mrs. Lightbear is very smart.

One of these sentences implies something about Mrs. Lightbear without using the words "like" or "as."

Example 2

2 **Which sentence includes a metaphor?**

A   Yoshe is skinny.

B   Martine dances beautifully, like a ballerina.

C   Kavi is a weasel.

D   Jamar drives like a cheetah.

Only one of these sentences implies
something by saying one thing is another.

Example 3

From her window, New York City sparkled like a jewel. Martine couldn't contain her excitement. She'd never been to a city. "I hope this is a good experience," she thought to herself. "I want to take it all in. See all the sights. I'm really lucky. I never thought I'd get here. Life really is a bowl of cherries."

3 **Which sentence includes a metaphor?**

A   "From her window, New York City
        sparkled like a jewel."

B   " 'I want to take it all in.' "

C   " 'I hope this is a good experience.' "

D   " 'Life really is a bowl of cherries.' "

One of these sentences compares two things
without using "like" or "as."

Like metaphors, **similes** compare two different things. Similes are usually easy to spot because they're explicit, meaning the author practically comes out and says, "Now I'm comparing two things." How? By using the words "like" or "as." That's one basic way metaphors and similes differ.

Usually with similes, authors compare something you don't know to something you do know, so you'll better understand what they're trying to describe. Look at the example below:

> Yoshe's parents peered down at her from the upstairs landing. The rest of the children at the birthday party were singing and talking as they danced wildly to the music. Yoshe, though, stood by herself in a corner, talking to no one. "I hope everything's all right with her," her mother thought worriedly. "That child is as quiet as a mouse."

Does Yoshe's mother mean that Yoshe is literally a mouse? Does she mean to imply that she squeaks? No. But most of us have an idea what a mouse is like. Yoshe's mother compares her daughter to a mouse so we'll get the idea that the girl makes very little noise, just as a mouse makes very little noise.

Like metaphors, similes often include some degree of exaggeration.

> When Kavi opened the door, he turned as white as a ghost.

In this example, it's unlikely that Kavi turned perfectly white. But he probably did lose color in his face. To say he turned "as white as a ghost" is an exaggeration.

When you read, remember that a sentence isn't automatically a simile if it includes "like" or "as." The sentence must compare two different things.

Read the sentence below, and then answer the question that follows.

The baby's hair was as soft as the fleece of a lamb.

What makes this sentence a simile?

_____

_____

_____

> **HINT** Using the word "like" or "as," similes compare two different things to give us a very vivid picture.

Example 4

Read this passage, and then answer the question that follows.

The mountains came out of nowhere. Their peaks jutted into the sky. It was as if someone had placed them there to keep out intruders. They were like a huge line of sentries. And there, between them and me, lay Lake Placid. It was perfectly flat and shimmered brightly.

 4 Which sentence includes a simile?

A "Their peaks jutted into the sky."

B "The mountains came out of nowhere."

C "They were like a huge line of sentries."

D "And there, between them and me, lay Lake Placid."

 Only one of these sentences uses "like" or "as" to compare two different things.

Example 5

5 **Which sentence includes a simile?**

A   The water rose as high as it could go.

B   She sings like an angel.

C   I really like when I'm by myself.

D   It was as if she'd never left.

Only one of the sentences uses "like" or "as" to compare two different things.

Example 6

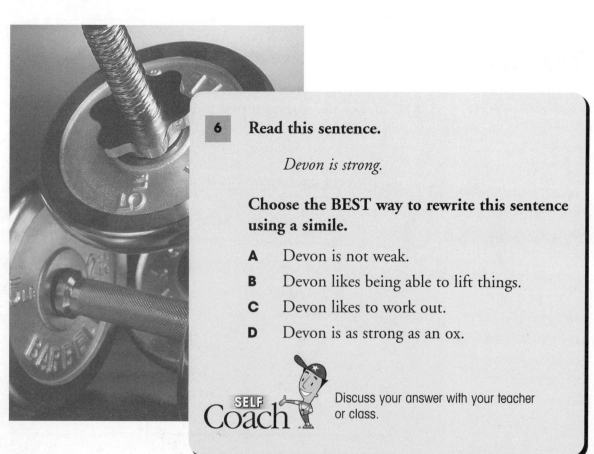

6 **Read this sentence.**

Devon is strong.

Choose the BEST way to rewrite this sentence using a simile.

A   Devon is not weak.

B   Devon likes being able to lift things.

C   Devon likes to work out.

D   Devon is as strong as an ox.

Discuss your answer with your teacher or class.

Standards: S2.I.1.C Identify significant literary elements (including metaphor, symbolism, foreshadowing, dialect, rhyme, meter, irony, climax) and use those elements to interpret the work.

S2.I.1.D Recognize different levels of meaning.

Lesson 7
Symbolism

What does a red rose symbolize? A dove? The U.S. flag? **Symbolism** is the use of something concrete to stand for something more abstract. A concrete thing is something you can touch or at least see, like a rose or a dove. An abstract thing is something you can't touch or see, like love or peace. We see symbols every day, all around us. Authors use them a lot. Sometimes they use common ones, like roses, doves, and flags, which already have certain meanings. Sometimes they make up their own symbols.

In either case, a symbol in a piece of writing is always an object. In other words, if you wanted to use the dove as a symbol of peace, you couldn't have it land on the dinner table in the winter or appear in somebody's hospital room. It still has to act like a dove.

Writers tend to develop symbols carefully. When looking for symbolism in a poem or story, ask yourself, "Does an object in this work appear often or seem important to the story?" If it does, it may be a symbol. Then you have to identify that idea. Symbols that seem simple may be hiding much deeper meanings.

Read the passage below, and then answer the question that follows.

Luis and Margot were driving across the desert when their car broke down. They had no cell phone and no way to fix their vehicle, so they decided to head out on foot. As they walked, they saw a vulture circling overhead. "Let's keep moving," Luis said, discouraging his friend from looking up. The two continued until they came upon a small gas station. There, a mechanic agreed to fix their vehicle. The vulture, though, was still overhead. Noticing Margot's look, the mechanic said, "Don't worry—They won't eat you folks for dinner tonight."

What is the symbol in this passage? What is its meaning?

_____

_____

_____

 Which object seems important to the characters?

Example 1

In 1778, New York State officially adopted its coat of arms. In the center are ships on the Hudson River. Grassy shores form the border. In the background, the sun rises behind a mountain range. There is a statue on either side of this scene. Both stand under an American eagle that's perched on a globe.

At the feet of the statue to the left is a discarded crown. This crown represents England, which used to rule New York. The statue to the right wears a blindfold and carries the scales of justice.

Beneath this whole scene is a white ribbon, which carries the state's motto: "Excelsior." It's meant to inspire all New Yorkers to reach for higher goals.

1a **What does the statue to the right symbolize?**

A   game playing

B   slavery

C   blindness

D   equal laws

Think about which of these represents an abstract idea that makes sense.

1b **The eagle is included because it represents**

F   wildlife

G   freedom

H   hunting

J   birds

Think about whether you have seen the eagle used before. What has it meant?

Example 2

The one-dollar bill, the way you know it today, rolled fresh off the presses in 1957. To some, it's just a piece of paper. But to others, it's a whole lot more.

Take the back of the bill, for example. There you'll find two circles. Together, the circles compose the Great Seal of the United States. Many years ago, when this country was young, the First Continental Congress asked Benjamin Franklin and a group of men to come up with a seal, a way to represent the new nation. It took them four years to decide on a seal and another two to get it approved. Franklin always believed one person couldn't do it alone, but many people, as a group, could.

In the left-hand circle of the seal is a pyramid. At the top of the pyramid is one all-seeing eye. The western side of the pyramid is dark, while its eastern side is light. When the seal was made, our country's founders hadn't yet explored the West. They left the pyramid open to show that the country had not done everything it could yet.

2a **The eye in the face is meant to symbolize**

   A   the ability to see all things

   B   Benjamin Franklin

   C   poor vision

   D   the group who made the seal

Remember that a symbol is meant to represent an idea you cannot touch.

2b **Why did the seal makers leave the top of the pyramid open?**

   F   They wanted to show that their work as a country wasn't done.

   G   They wanted to make room for the all-seeing eye.

   H   They didn't have time to finish it.

   J   They wanted to show you could put things in it.

Discuss your answer with your teacher or class.

Standard: S2.I.1.C Identify significant literary elements (including metaphor, symbolism, foreshadowing, dialect, rhyme, meter, irony, climax) and use those elements to interpret the work.

Lesson 8
Irony

Like metaphors, similes, and symbols, irony is something authors use to make their writing more interesting and colorful. Authors who use **irony** let you in on something the characters don't know. That information changes the way you see the story. Sometimes, authors make characters say one thing but mean another. When they are doing this, they are using an *ironic* tone, or being sarcastic.

> Darnell clutched his seat as the room spun. All around him was pandemonium. "You won!" screamed his wife. "You won, you won! After all these years, you finally won the lottery!" Slowly, the room came to a halt, and Darnell cleared his head. "Aren't you going to say something, Darnell?" his wife asked. Darnell was beaming from ear to ear. "I know—we're rich, and I'll never have to work again! This is awful!"

Does he really mean winning the lottery is awful? No. It's ironic for Darnell to say something like that with a grin, because he means the opposite. He thinks winning the lottery is wonderful. He'll never have to work again.

Often, authors use irony to express humor. Think about how much more interesting and entertaining a story is when something happens you didn't expect. Imagine, for example, that a man cancels a date with his girlfriend to go out with friends, only to see his girlfriend while he's out. The man can get into a lot of funny situations trying to avoid his girlfriend.

In the dark theater, Marisol could feel her throat tighten. She knew the movie's hero didn't commit the crime, but now she was going to pay for it. Her enemy would see to it. "This shouldn't be too bad," the hero said as she entered the courtroom. Marisol's throat tightened even more.

What is the irony in the movie in this passage?

_____

_____

_____

HINT! What the hero says takes on new meaning, because Marisol knows something she doesn't.

Example 1

Yoshe couldn't help it—the sly smile wouldn't come off her face. "This time," she thought, "I'm really going to surprise my parents."

For weeks, she'd been planning to buy these movie tickets. Since the moment she'd first seen the billboard saying "Class Act: The Sound of Music," she knew she had to get tickets for her parents. Classical music wasn't her favorite, but her parents played it non-stop. Much to Yoshe's dismay, they even played it in the car.

Now, as Yoshe stood waiting for her parents, she could barely contain herself. She turned to the boy next to her.

"Are you here to see the movie, too?" she asked. "Are you a fan of classical music?"

It was clear from his expression that the boy was confused. "Uh, what are you talking about?" he asked Yoshe with a frown. "I'm here to see the movie, but it's about the rock band, Class Act. And they're far from classical. They're more like heavy metal."

Yoshe's heart sank as her parents arrived.

"Want to go inside?" Yoshe's mother asked as she drew closer.

"Oh, yes," Yoshe replied. "Now I really can't wait to get inside."

1a **The irony is this passage is that**

A the boy misunderstood Yoshe

B Yoshe planned one thing but another happened

C the boy doesn't like classical music

D Yoshe bought tickets but doesn't like classical music

In this passage, the expected results and actual ones differ.

1b **Which of the following is an example of an ironic tone?**

F "They're more like heavy metal."

G "Uh, what are you talking about?"

H "Now I really can't wait to get inside."

J "Want to go inside?"

In one of these examples, the speaker says one thing but means the opposite.

Example 2

"Now, Jamar, where are you going?" Mrs. Lightbear asked as the boy ran ahead of the group. Turning around, Jamar smoothed his jacket and replied, "Just showing off my new windbreaker. I've been waiting to wear it all year. Don't be jealous," he said impishly. "If you get cold, maybe I'll let you wear it." The rest of the group laughed.

Despite herself, Mrs. Lightbear laughed, too. "Well, it's very cold and windy today. I'll give you that," she admitted.

Soon, the children starting setting up for lunch. The wind, though, showed no signs of letting up. Soon the skies darkened. Mrs. Lightbear was too busy to notice when the first white flakes started hitting the ground. Then one hit her boot, and she looked up, clearly shocked.

Looking around, Mrs. Lightbear noticed Jamar shivering. "Oh, my, Jamar—let's get you warm." "Yeah, I'm frozen," the boy replied, "I'm really glad I have this windbreaker now."

2a **When Jamar says, "I'm really glad I have this windbreaker now," he means**

A he is not happy he has his windbreaker now

B his windbreaker has kept him very warm

C he got his windbreaker just in time

D he is happy to wear his windbreaker

Think about whether Jamar means exactly what he says.

2b **What is the irony in this passage?**

F Mrs. Lightbear was too busy to notice the snowstorm.

G Jamar got very cold in his windbreaker, which he originally wore with pride.

H Jamar wore his windbreaker in time for a snowstorm.

J Mrs. Lightbear noticed that Jamar was cold.

Discuss your answer with your teacher or class.

Lesson 9
Rhyme and Meter

As you learned in Lesson 1, poetry has some essential features. It's broken into lines and stanzas, and it uses rhythm and sometimes rhyme.

Words that **rhyme** sound alike. "Duck," "stuck," and "luck" rhyme. This means they sound the same. When a poem uses rhyme, its lines end with words that sound alike. Those words often appear at the end of every line or at the end of every other line. Read these lines:

I Wish Today Were Yesterday

1. I do not care, I did not care,
2. I will not care tomorrow
3. I only want to laugh and play—
4. Now hear my tale of sorrow.

In this poem, the rhyming words "tomorrow" and "sorrow" appear at the ends of every other line.

Poetry may also use rhythm. **Rhythm** is the way the lines in a poem sound when you read them. **Meter** is the pattern of that rhythm. You can figure out meter by seeing which syllables are stressed, or spoken more forcefully, in each line of the poem. Look at this example:

At the Sea-side, by Robert Louis Stevenson

1. When **I** was **down** be**side** the **sea**
2. A **woo**den **spade** they **gave** to **me**
3. To **dig** the **san**dy **shore**.

In each line, the words or parts of words that are stressed appear in bold. So take Line 1, for example. There are seven words, but when you say this line out loud, you hear eight sounds, or beats. Every other beat is louder than the rest because it's stressed.

Poetry is a very expressive type of writing. It's meant to make you feel a certain way. Things like rhyme and meter help poets express their feelings, and they give poems an almost song-like quality that make them stand out from other kinds of writing.

Example 1

From **The Raven**, by Edgar Allen Poe

1. Once upon a midnight dreary, while I pondered, weak and weary,
2. Over many a quaint and curious volume of forgotten lore,
3. While I nodded, nearly napping, suddenly there came a tapping,
4. As of some one gently rapping, rapping at my chamber door.
5. "Tis some visitor," I muttered, "tapping at my chamber door—
6. Only this, and nothing more."

1a **Which words from this poem do not rhyme?**

A "dreary" and "weary"

B "lore" and "door"

C "nodded" and "napping"

D "napping" and "tapping"

 Words that rhyme sound alike.

1b **Which set of lines has the same meter?**

F 1 and 3

G 2 and 6

H 1 and 6

J 3 and 4

 One line has far fewer beats than the others, while the rest of the lines are separated by just one beat.

Example 2

From **The Crocus**, by Harriet Beecher Stowe

1. Around the soft, green swelling mound
2. We scooped the earth away,
3. And buried deep the crocus-bulbs
4. Against a coming day.
5. These roots are dry, and brown, and sere;
6. Why plant them here? he said,
7. To leave them, all the winter long,
8. So desolate and dead.

2a **How many beats are there in Line 4?**

- A 3
- B 6
- C 5
- D 8

The number of beats is the number of sounds in a line, not the number of words.

2b **Which set of lines from this poem rhyme?**

- F 1 and 2
- G 1 and 3
- H 2 and 4
- J 5 and 6

Discuss your answer with your teacher or class.

Standards: S2.I.1.C Identify significant literary elements (including metaphor, symbolism, foreshadowing, dialect, rhyme, meter, irony, climax) and use those elements to interpret the work.

S2.I.1.D Recognize different levels of meaning.

Coached Reading

The following passage is about a boy and his mother. As you read the passage and the accompanying poem, use the statements and questions in the margin to help your understanding.

 Your teacher may read this selection to you.

"I know camp is only for the summer," the mother said sadly as she watched her son pack his room. "I know it'll be over soon. But you never used to go for the whole summer. You used to only want to go for a week or two, at the most. You're not even gone yet, and I already miss you. It's too quiet. This house is a morgue without you."

> Where is there an example of a metaphor? What makes it a metaphor?

At first, the boy didn't respond to his mother's words, though his shoulders stooped and he paused. Putting his favorite stuffed dog, now dirty and worn, into a box, finally he turned toward her. "Come on, Mom. You know it's not nearly that bad," he said in a reassuring tone. "You still have Dad, and all the animals. The place isn't a morgue when I'm not here. This house is more like a zoo!"

> Is there an example of simile here? Circle the clue.

Sadly, the mother smiled. She even managed a half-hearted laugh. "You just grew up too fast," she sighed as she reached to retrieve the boy's worn dog from its box. She held the toy close and fondled its ears and back. "I'm sorry, I just can't help but be very sad," she said. "It seems like just a few days ago you were dragging this dog everywhere, and now you're packing it away. Things won't ever be the same again."

"Come on, Mom," the boy tried again, taking the dog from his mother and returning it to its box. "I'll be back soon—I promise. I'll call and e-mail all the time. When I get back we'll have dinner, go to the movies, just like old times. It'll be like nothing has changed."

"Yeah, right," said the mother, unconvinced. "Nothing has changed. Just that my little boy is leaving me—and growing up and putting away all his toys."

Remembering something, suddenly the mother brightened a little. "Wait a second," she said, "I'll be right back." After a few minutes, she returned to the boy's room with a sheet of paper clutched in her hand. "Here," she said offering the paper to her son, "take this to camp and read it when you can. It's one of my favorite poems. It expresses just how I feel."

What do you think the toy dog symbolizes? What does it mean to the boy's mother?

Does the mother really mean that nothing has changed? What is this an example of?

Little Boy Blue

adapted from the poem by Eugene Field

1. The little toy dog is covered with dust,
2. But sturdy and staunch he stands;
3. And the little toy soldier is red with rust,
4. And the musket molds in his hands.

5. Time was when the little toy dog was new,
6. And the soldier was passing fair;
7. And that was the time when our Little Boy Blue
8. Kissed them and put them there.

9. "Now, don't you go till I come," he said,
10. "And don't you make any noise!"
11. So, toddling off to his trundle-bed,
12. He dreamt of the pretty toys;

13. And, as he was dreaming, an angel song
14. Awakened our Little Boy Blue—
15. Oh! the years are many, the years are long,
16. But the little toy friends are true!

17. Aye, faithful to Little Boy Blue they stand,
18. Each in the same old place—
19. Awaiting the touch of a little hand,
20. The smile of a little face;

21. And they wonder, as waiting the long years through
22. In the dust of that little chair,
23. What has become of our Little Boy Blue,
24. Since he kissed them and put them there.

What do you notice about the meter of this poem? Which lines have the same kind of rhythm?

How does the poet use rhyme here? Circle the words that sound alike.

Is the number of beats consistent from line to line? Can you recognize a general pattern? What is the pattern? Circle the sounds that are stressed.

Reread the passage, and ask yourself the questions in the margin again. Then, do Numbers 1 through 6.

1 Which of the following is an example of a simile?

A "The little toy dog is covered with dust."

B "This house is more like a zoo!"

C "It'll be like nothing has changed."

D "I know camp is only for the summer."

2 Lines 10 and 12 of the poem have the same meter because they have

F words that sound alike

G the same number of words

H the same number of beats

J words that are the same length

3 What does the boy's toy dog symbolize in this passage? Write your answer on the lines below.

_____

_____

_____

4 The boy's mother uses a metaphor when she says

A "This house is a morgue without you."

B "I know it'll be over soon."

C "I just can't help but be very sad."

D "You just grew up too fast."

5 Which of the following words from the poem rhyme?

F "noise" and "bed"

G "said" and "bed"

H "said" and "noise"

J "noise" and "song"

6 What does the mother mean when she says "Nothing has changed"? Why is this an example of an ironic tone? Write your answer on the lines below.

_____

_____

_____

Discuss your answer with your teacher or class.

Test Practice

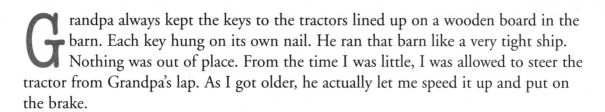

Read the following passage about a girl and her grandfather. Then do Numbers 1 through 4.

Grandpa always kept the keys to the tractors lined up on a wooden board in the barn. Each key hung on its own nail. He ran that barn like a very tight ship. Nothing was out of place. From the time I was little, I was allowed to steer the tractor from Grandpa's lap. As I got older, he actually let me speed it up and put on the brake.

But I was never allowed to touch the keys. Grandpa got them down from their posts, Grandpa started the tractor, Grandpa returned them to their place after work. This summer when I showed up on the farm, Grandpa gave me a big hug, then looked me over.

"You're getting pretty tall," he said. "How old are you now?"

"Thirteen, Grandpa," I said. "In the fall, I start eighth grade."

"Wow," he replied. "You're a very adult woman. You know what? I think you're getting so tall you can reach that board over there." He pointed to the board that held the tractor keys.

"I sure can," I said.

Did he really want me to get the keys? "We'll be using the—" he started.

"I know, Grandpa: the 3088."

"Right," he smiled. "Grab the key, and let's get going."

"Right," I said as I stood and lifted the key off the hook, acting like it was no big deal. Really, it was like heaven for me.

1 The key in this passage represents

A   Grandpa

B   adulthood

C   youth

D   farming

2 Which of the following is a simile?

F   "But I was never allowed to touch the keys."

G   "Nothing was out of place."

H   "He ran that barn like a very tight ship."

J   "It was Grandpa who would get them down from their posts."

3 Which of the following is an example of irony?

A   "How old are you now?"

B   "In the fall, I start eighth grade."

C   "You're a very adult woman."

D   "I sure can."

4 What is the metaphor in this passage? What makes it a metaphor? How would you rewrite the passage to add another one?

_____

_____

_____

_____

_____

_____

_____

_____

_____

_____

_____

_____

_____

_____

_____

_____

_____

_____

_____

_____

NOTICE: Photocopying any part of this book is forbidden by law.

107

Read the following passage about a boy and his friend. Then do Numbers 5 through 8.

"You know," Jason said, "you really have two choices. You can either give us the answers to the test, or not. But if you don't, don't expect us to hang out with you anymore."

"Gee, thanks. That's really kind," Hector replied. "I can either do something wrong, or lose people I thought were my friends. Doesn't seem like much of a choice to me."

"Well, you know, Hector," Jason continued, "life's really all about choices. Good ones and bad ones. Don't you remember that poem we read in class last week—that one by Robert Frost? It's like that."

He took his book out of his bag and read.

1. Two Roads diverged in a yellow wood,
2. And sorry that I could not travel both
3. And be one traveler, long I stood
4. And looked down one as far as I could
5. To where it bent in the undergrowth;
6. Then took the other, as just as fair,
7. And having perhaps the better claim,
8. Because it was grassy and wanted wear;
9. Though as for that the passing there
10. Had worn them really about the same. . .

5 How many beats does Line 5 have?

F   6

G   7

H   8

J   9

6 Which set of lines in the poem rhyme?

A   4 and 5

B   5 and 6

C   6 and 7

D   6 and 8

7 The two paths in the poem symbolize

F   friends

G   options

H   maps

J   trails

8 When Hector says, "Gee, thanks. That's really kind," what does he really mean? What is this an example of?

_____

_____

_____

CHAPTER

3

Part 2: Putting it to Use

Writing from the Imagination

Lesson 10: Writing a Short Story

In Chapter 1, you learned about the things that make up a good story, like plot, character, setting, and theme. When you write a story, you have to remember to include all these things. If they're not there, the reader may not keep reading your story.

When you write a story, think about the basic things you need to include in your story to make it believable, as well as the things that will keep your readers interested, and continue reading.

Let's get started writing a short story. Trying to write a short story will make you a better reader of stories, and it could help you on your English Language Arts test.

Example 1

> **Sketch out the main character in your story. Be sure to think about how the main character speaks and acts. Does your character get along well with other people? Does your character have a trait, or quality, that makes him or her special? Remember, your main character doesn't have to be a hero. Consider making the main character evil or comical.**
>
> _____
>
> _____
>
> _____
>
> _____
>
> _____

Example 2

Think up a plot for a simple short story, being sure to include conflict, rising action, climax, and resolution. As you do, think about how you'll introduce your story. Think of ways to include foreshadowing. How will you let your readers know what will happen?

_____

_____

_____

_____

_____

_____

_____

_____

_____

_____

Example 3

Using the plot you developed, decide on the setting of your story. Be sure to include when and where the story occurs. Try to think of really vivid details and interesting ways to reveal the setting.

_____

_____

_____

_____

_____

Example 4

Finally, identify the theme of your story. What message would you like your readers to take away? If you need to, go back and rethink your plot. When you do, think about using symbols to support your theme.

_____

_____

_____

Example 5

Now it's time to put it all together. Write a story using the plot, setting, characters, and theme you've developed. Be sure to:

- include all parts of the plot, using foreshadowing when possible
- make your characters act and speak like real people
- use vivid detail to describe the environment and the people
- try to use things like metaphors, similes, symbols, and irony to make your story more interesting

Start the story below, and then use your own paper to complete it.

_____

_____

_____

_____

_____

_____

_____

_____

_____

_____

_____

_____

_____

_____

_____

_____

_____

Standards: S2.I.2.C   Write stories, poems, literary essays, and plays that observe the conventions of the genre and contain interesting and effective language and voice.

S2.I.2.D   Use standard English effectively.

Lesson 11
Writing a Poem

Poetry is perhaps the most creative form of writing. Poets use figures of speech, like metaphors and similes, to express their feelings. And they use lines of text that have rhythm and often rhyme.

But poetry doesn't always have to rhyme or have a regular rhythm. Some poems have regular rhythms but no rhyme and some have neither. Haiku is one type of poem that doesn't rhyme, but it does have very specific requirements for form. A **haiku** is a very old form of Japanese poetry that has only three lines and seventeen syllables total. The syllables are broken up in the lines as follows:

Line 1 has five syllables

Line 2 has seven syllables

Line 3 has five syllables

In a haiku, the first line ends after the fifth syllable, as it does in the following example:

> Cheerful old squatters,
> Poems occupy my brain
> And refuse to leave.

Read the passage below, and then answer the question that follows.

Snow melts.
Suddenly, the village
is full of children.

How does this poem differ from a true haiku? How could you change it to make it fit the form?

_____

_____

_____

_____

HINT! A true haiku has five syllables on the first line and seven on the second.

Traditional haikus capture one moment in nature—like a picture or a painting. While traditional haikus are about things like the seasons, they can be about anything—as long as they express emotion. With very few words, a haiku poem catches the reader's attention and says, "Think about this."

Writing a poem might help you enjoy reading poems.

Example 1

During recess, a hike, or a family trip, record something you observe. It can be anything—leaves blowing in the wind, ducks swimming in a pond, insects buzzing around a light.

_____

_____

_____

Example 2

Next, try to think of something else you saw, something related to the item you recorded in the last example and something you think will make a lasting impression. An example might be that there were turtles sunning themselves near the ducks.

_____

_____

_____

_____

Example 3

Now you have the material you need to write a haiku. Remember to follow haiku convention: a haiku has only three lines and seventeen syllables. Using the material in the previous examples, you might write a haiku like this:

> The turtles watch as
> the poor ducks swim and paddle
> to the other shore.

Now try it yourself using your material.

_____

_____

_____

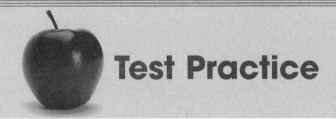

Test Practice

Write a short story about a person who must find a way to complete a tough neighborhood project. You can use what you wrote in Lesson 10 (or a version of it), or start something new. Make sure to include an authority figure—a parent, a teacher, a policeman, a neighbor—anyone you want. And remember that your main character doesn't have to be a hero. Consider making the main character a villain, or a clown. Your story can be nonfiction—about something that happened to you or a friend. Use the Editing Checklist on page 119 to check your writing.

Make sure your story has

- a clear plot that includes conflict, rising action, climax, and resolution
- characters who act and speak like real people
- a setting described in vivid detail
- a theme, something you'd like your readers to take away

If you can, make the story more interesting by including foreshadowing, metaphors, similes, symbols, and irony.

You may PLAN your writing on this page if you wish, but do NOT write your final story on this page. Write your final story on pages 118 and 119. You may need to continue the story on your own paper.

Answer

_____

_____

_____

_____

_____

_____

_____

_____

_____

_____

_____

_____

_____

_____

_____

_____

_____

Editing Checklist

1 Check your capitalization and punctuation.

2 Spell all words correctly.

3 Check for sentence fragments and run-on sentences.

4 Keep verb tense consistent.

5 Make sure subjects and verbs agree.

6 Use words according to the rules of standard English.

7 Remember to break paragraphs correctly.

Write a haiku about the summer. Don't use what you wrote in Lesson 11—start something new. Try to remember the things you saw, the things you did—even the things you heard and smelled. Remember that the main point of a haiku is to make an impression. Think about those things that made an impression on you.

When you get ready to start writing, make sure your haiku has

- an observation, preferably about nature
- an idea that relates to your observation
- only three lines and seventeen syllables

You may PLAN your writing on this page if you wish, but do NOT write your final haiku on this page. Write your final haiku on page 121. If you like your haiku, you may write more than one.

UNIT

2 Reading and Writing Nonfiction

GETTING THE IDEA

There's a world of factual information out there, so how do you find your way through it?

Step by step, this unit will guide you, kicking off its tour with explanations of textbooks and reference materials. Once you've had a chance to make the most of those, you'll move on to things like charts, graphics, and taking notes. Then, you'll move on to the finer points of reading. You'll learn about format, sequence—even how people speak!

But there's far more to this tour. It's just getting started. Before you're through, you'll pick up on context, make inferences, and appreciate authors' points of view. Then you'll move on to the next steps: understanding what you're reading and using what you know. You'll compare and contrast, and you'll delve into details.

Then, armed with all this, you'll launch into writing yourself. First, you'll understand the process, then, you'll try it out. Only after all this will you come to the end. With luck, and this unit's practice, you should have better listening and reading skills.

Standards: S1.I.1.A Interpret and analyze information from textbooks and nonfiction books for young adults, reference materials, audio and media presentations, oral interviews, graphs, charts, diagrams, and electronic databases intended for a general audience.

S1.I.1.B Compare and synthesize information from different sources.

S3.I.1.A Analyze, interpret, and evaluate information, ideas, organization, and language from academic and nonacademic texts, such as textbooks, public documents, book and movie reviews, and editorials.

CHAPTER 4

Part 1: Reading to Discover

Using Nonfiction

Lesson 12: Reading Your Textbook for Information

Depending on the information you're after—whether it's background material, current events, or entertainment—there are different kinds of materials you can turn to. **Textbooks** provide factual information. Textbooks are meant to explain things so you can understand and learn from them. They group information into chapters.

As you'll see in Chapter 5, textbooks have certain tools in the front and back—things like tables of contents and indexes—that help guide you to the correct information. Inside each chapter, textbooks have other types of tools to guide you. Look at the following example from a textbook on New York history:

The Erie Canal— America's First Superhighway

The **Main Heading** tells you what this part of the book is about.

Long before millions of cars raced down the highway, New York had its own "superhighway," but it wasn't like the highways you know today. It was a water one, and it was called the Erie Canal.

Breaking New Ground

Subheadings like this describe small sections of the book.

When it opened in 1825, the Erie Canal was a marvel of engineering and human labor. From Albany to Buffalo, it opened up the American frontier and made westward expansion inevitable. It turned New York Harbor into the nation's number one port. It shaped social and economic development. Cities and industries developed along the canal and flourished.

Before the Canal

Until the American colonies declared independence in 1776, European settlement of the New World was largely confined to the eastern seaboard. The Appalachian Mountains were a formidable obstacle to westward movement. Only the Mohawk River Valley in New York offered both a land and a water passage through the mountains.

How the Canal Came to Be

By 1817, plans for a human-made waterway fed by the Mohawk River that bypassed its waterfalls and rapids had been made. This plan created the Erie Canal, which connected Albany and the Hudson River in the east with Buffalo and the Great Lakes in the west.

When it was completed in 1825, the Erie Canal traversed New York. It turned New York Harbor into America's number one port, and it shaped the social and economic development of the nation. Shipping costs dropped dramatically. Immigrants to America, in search of new lands and new opportunities in the west, crowded canal boats. Cities and industries along the canal developed and flourished. The Erie Canal brought prosperity to Syracuse and to America.

Illustrations help explain information in visual ways.

NOTICE: Photocopying any part of this book is forbidden by law.

125

Textbooks use features like headings and illustrations to help guide you and to highlight or summarize certain information. Illustrations are a particularly helpful feature of textbooks if you're a visual learner—that is, if you learn better when you see something.

Example 1

All about Galaxies

Have you ever looked up at night and seen faintly shining lights? You may have seen a galaxy! A galaxy is a collection of gas, dust, and stars held together by a force called gravity. Gravity pulls objects together. When many objects the same size come together, they tend to stay together thanks to gravity. A galaxy is like a huge island of stars in outer space.

Galaxies are named for their shapes. A spiral galaxy, for example, is shaped like a flat disk with a bump in the middle. From the top, it looks like a pinwheel. It has bright spiral arms that curl out from the center. The Milky Way, which is home to our planet Earth, is an example of a spiral galaxy. Other galaxies lack spiral arms and are much rounder. Some galaxies have no clear shapes at all.

1a **A good subheading for this passage would be**

A   "The Shape of Earth"

B   "How to Eat a Milky Way"

C   "The Shapes of Galaxies"

D   "Fun Things to Do with Gravity"

1b **Which of the following would be another good illustration for this passage?**

F   a map of the earth

G   a photograph of a lightbulb

H   a picture of a candy bar

J   a diagram of a spiral

Discuss your answer with your teacher or class.

Standards: S1.I.1.A Interpret and analyze information from textbooks and nonfiction books for young adults, reference materials, audio and media presentations, oral interviews, graphs, charts, diagrams, and electronic databases intended for a general audience.

S1.I.1.B Compare and synthesize information from different sources.

Lesson 13
Reading Other
Reference Materials

Like textbooks, which you learned about in Lesson 12, **magazines** are resources you can turn to when reading for information. Also like textbooks, magazines have tables of contents you can scan to find the information that interests you. Magazines generally group information into articles.

While textbooks and magazines have similarities, they differ, too. Magazines, for example, are published more often and usually have features, or columns, that appear in every issue. A woodworking magazine might have a regular feature called "Tips from Readers," for example, while a fishing magazine might have a regular column called "Ask the Angler." When you read more than one issue of a magazine, you'll start to see a pattern.

Keep in mind that magazines are one type of publication that may try to persuade you—and they sometimes try to entertain you. Textbooks, on the other hand, won't try to do that. Textbooks are purely informational. As an example, look at the magazine article on the next page.

The STATUE OF LIBERTY Gets a *Facelift*!

By Laticia Adams and Smokey Peters

Well, it's about time, we do declare! Our lady of the ocean, our Statue of Liberty, is going to get a facelift! And just in time for her hundredth birthday!

A Long and Successful History

The Statue of Liberty National Monument officially celebrated her 100th birthday on October 28, 1986. The people of France gave the statue to the people of the United States over 100 years ago in recognition of the friendship established during the American Revolution. Over the years, the Statue of Liberty has grown to symbolize freedom and democracy as well as this international friendship.

Sculptor Frederic Auguste Bartholdi was commissioned to design a sculpture with the year 1876 in mind for completion, to commemorate the centennial of the American Declaration of Independence. The statue was a joint effort between America and France and it was agreed that the American people would build the pedestal and the French people would be responsible for the statue and its assembly here in the United States.

The Statue Hits a Few Bumps

However, lack of funds was a problem on both sides of the Atlantic Ocean. In France, public fees, various forms of entertainment, and a lottery were among the methods used to raise funds. In America, fund raising for the pedestal was going particularly slowly, so Joseph Pulitzer (noted for the Pulitzer Prize) opened up the editorial pages of his newspaper, the *World* to support the fund raising effort. Pulitzer used his newspaper to criticize both the rich who had failed to finance the pedestal construction and the middle class who were content to rely upon the wealthy to provide the funds. Pulitzer's campaign of harsh criticism was successful in motivating the people of America to donate.

The Statue Finds Her Place—and New Face

After challenges like these were overcome, on October 28, 1886, the dedication of the Statue of Liberty took place in front of thousands of spectators. She was a centennial gift 10 years late. Now, 100 years later, the Statue of Liberty is showing her age, so she's getting a little update—a facelift of sorts.

In May 1982, President Ronald Reagan appointed Lee Iacocca to head up a private-sector effort to restore the Statue of Liberty. Fundraising began for the $87 million restoration under a public/private partnership between the National Park Service and the Statue of Liberty-Ellis Island Foundation, Inc., to date the most successful such partnership in American history. In 1984, at the start of the statue's restoration, the United Nations designated the Statue of Liberty a World Heritage Site. On July 5, 1986, the newly restored statue reopened to the public during Liberty Weekend, which celebrated her centennial.

So the statue may have been a little late, but now she's looking brand new.

Additional research by Constance Roberts.

> Sometimes, additional information like this will appear at the end of an article.

> Like textbooks, magazines can include illustrations or pictures to share information.

About Town—New York's Magazine
December 28, 1986

December 28, 1986
About Town—New York's Magazine

> You can find the name of the magazine, and sometimes the date, at the bottom of the page.

Example 1

Riverbank's Carousel of Dreams

By Maxwell Groban

Ever been to Riverbank State Park in New York City? Well, then, you're really missing something. Not only is it the only park of its kind in the Western Hemisphere, it's home to a carousel of dreams.

Perched on the banks of the Hudson River, Riverside's got many things to offer. It's got a skating rink, a roller rink, a sports complex, and even a restaurant. But one thing really stands out at the park: the Totally Kid Carousel.

In 1993, a man named Milo Mottola was picked to plan a carousel for the park. Remembering that carousels are really for kids, he asked the kids in his Harlem neighborhood for ideas. "I knew they'd have the best ones," he said.

As it turns out, he was right. The children made drawings of all kinds of things—there were more than 1,000 drawings in all. What Milo came up with is really unique. Instead of the usual ponies, this carousel has giant spiders, a plaid zebra, a kangaroo, and much more. But best of all, it's a place where kids can come for fun.

Additional research by Carla Montana

1a **The point of this article is to**

A   tell the story of how the carousel came to be

B   explain how to find Riverside Park

C   inform readers how to make a carousel

D   convince readers to build a carousel

1b **Which of the following would be a good sub-heading for this article?**

F   "Where to Put the Carousel"

G   "How the Carousel Got Its Start"

H   "Finding Fun in Harlem"

J   "Fun in the Palisades Mountains"

SELF Coach™

Discuss your answer with your teacher or class.

Standards: S1.I.1.A Interpret and analyze information from textbooks and nonfiction books for young adults, reference materials, audio and media presentations, oral interviews, graphs, charts, diagrams, and electronic databases intended for a general audience.

S1.I.1.B Compare and synthesize information from different sources.

Lesson 14
Reading Charts, Graphs, and Maps

Illustrations are a good way to help you understand information, especially if you learn best by seeing something. Resources like textbooks and magazines include things like charts, graphs, and maps that help you understand information.

Charts

A **chart** puts data into geometric shapes. Sometimes, a chart shows how one thing that happens leads to something else. Or it shows how things are organized.

Look at this organizational chart:

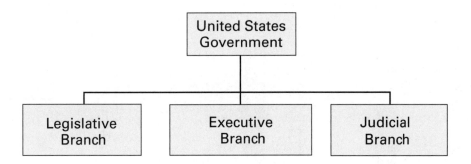

This chart shows the branches of the U.S. government. The top box represents the government as a whole, and the three boxes underneath each represent a branch. The three lower boxes are parts of the main box above.

THINKING IT THROUGH   Read the passage below, and then answer the question that follows.

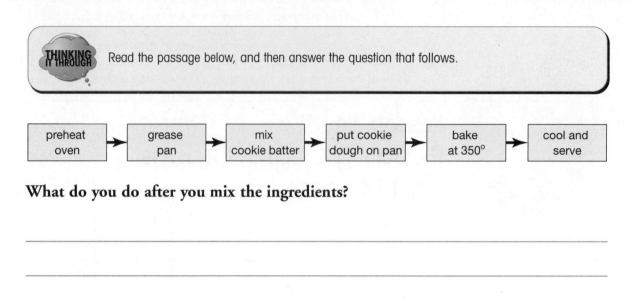

What do you do after you mix the ingredients?

_____

_____

_____

Graphs

A **graph** shows how two or more things relate. One of the most common graphs is the bar graph. For an example, look below:

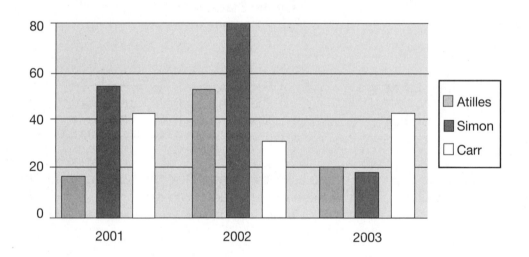

This bar graph shows the attendance records of three people in United States Congress, from 2001 to 2003. From this graph, you can see that Simon had the best attendance in 2001 and 2002, and that Carr had the best attendance in 2003.

Read the chart below, and then answer the question that follows.

Profit Record: Mrs. Terry's Cookie Company

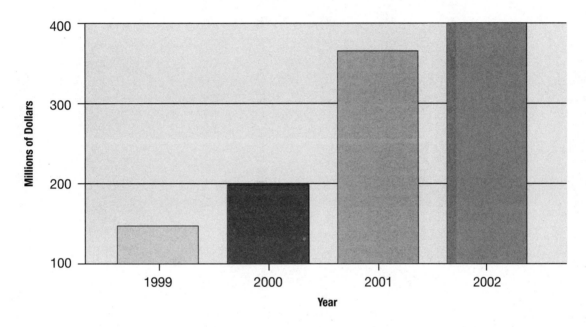

How much profit did Mrs. Terry's Cookie Company make in 2001?

_____

_____

_____

Maps show physical locations. There are many kinds of maps. Some maps show where cities and towns are located in states or countries. Some maps show how resources are distributed. Some maps show how to get from place to place. Look at the map of the United States below:

This map shows all the states in America, as well as where they're located relative to one another. New York, for example, is next to states like Pennsylvania and Vermont.

Read the passage below, and then answer the question that follows.

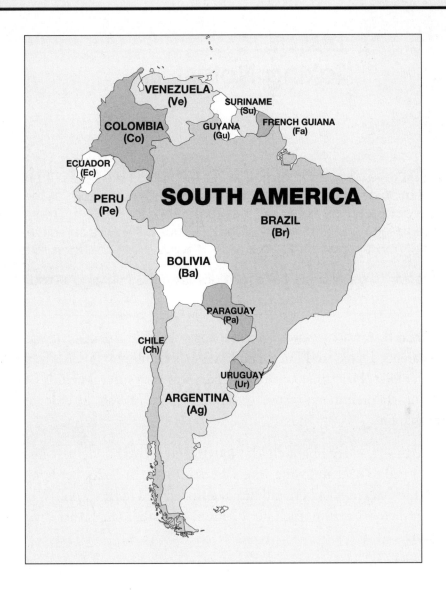

Which country in South America is the largest?

_____

_____

_____

Standard: S1.I.1.B Compare and synthesize information from different sources.

Lesson 15
Taking Notes

When you're reading for information, it's helpful to take notes. There's a lot of information out there, so it may be tempting to write down all the facts you come across. But try not to do this. Remember to weed out information that doesn't relate to the topic you're researching. Besides, if you're selective, and only record the facts most important to your topic, finding and using facts later will be easier.

Now you're ready to get started. Let's take notes on the following passage:

> Susan B. Anthony was born in February 1820 in Adams, Massachusetts. Her parents, Daniel and Lucy, had seven other children. Susan was the second oldest. Her father, a cotton maker, was very strict. He didn't allow his children to enjoy toys, games, or music. Instead, he enforced self-discipline.
>
> Susan was a very bright child, though, and thrived under self-discipline. She learned to read and write when she was three. In 1826, her family moved to Battensville, NY, and Susan enrolled in a local school. When the teacher there refused to teach her division, her father taught her division at home.

When you're taking notes on a passage like this, what's the first thing you should do? Write down the main topic of the passage. Then, look at the rest of the passage. Generally, a piece of writing breaks into paragraphs. Each paragraph will have a main idea and supporting facts. One good way to approach note taking is to list the main idea of a paragraph first. Then, write down each paragraph's important facts.

Here what notes for this passage might look like:

Susan B. Anthony

Early years

Born in 1820 in Massachusetts

Second of seven children

Strict father

Bright child

Learned to read at three

Went to district school in
New York

Learned long division at home

Notice some of the things that don't
appear. For example, we didn't take
down that Susan's father didn't let her
listen to music. The notation "strict father" implies that.
Remember that note-taking is just meant to capture the key points.

THINKING IT THROUGH

Read the passage below, and then answer the question that follows.

Antarctica, the coldest, most desolate place on Earth, is the continent surrounding the South Pole. It covers 5.4 million square miles and contains 90 percent of the world's ice. Much of that ice is one mile thick. Snow covers the ice. In the winter, the center of Antarctica dips to an extremely frigid –100 degrees Fahrenheit. On the coast, it's a bit warmer: –40 degrees Fahrenheit.

The only place where animals can survive in Antarctica is on the coast, where it's slightly warmer, or in the sea. Penguins, seals, whales, and other fish and birds all live in or close to the coastal waters.

How would you take notes on this passage? Write your notes on the lines below.

Standards: S1.I.1.A Interpret and analyze information from textbooks and nonfiction books for young adults, as well as reference materials, audio and media presentations, oral interviews, graphs, charts, diagrams, and electronic databases intended for a general audience.

S1.I.1.B Compare and synthesize information from different sources.

S3.I.1.A Analyze, interpret, and evaluate information, ideas, organization, and language from academic and nonacademic texts, such as textbooks, public documents, book and movie reviews, and editorials.

Coached Reading

The following passage is about the Amazon rain forest. As you read the passage, use the statements and questions in the margin to help your understanding.

 Your teacher may read this selection to you.

Alert—Save the Amazon!

by Leslie Best

Fierce piranhas and swift jaguars make their homes there. Brightly colored parrots flitter about, and monkeys swing from the trees. The Amazon is a wondrous place, but the Amazon rain forest is in danger of vanishing.

Flirting with Disaster

The lush Amazon rain forest stretches for about 2.7 million square miles. It holds one-fifth of the planet's supply of fresh water, and the world's largest variety of plant and animal life.

For many years, though, this place has been shrinking. Since the 1960s, loggers, miners, and farmers from Brazil and nearby countries have been moving into the Amazon. They've been destroying trees as they go. Some companies have cut trees for wood and paper. Others have burned trees to clear the land. Construction has destroyed millions of trees. Roads and airport runways now cross the landscape.

> What kind of writing does this seem to be?

> Can you think of a sub-heading to go here?

Confirming the Worst

In early 1998, the government in Brazil announced what many people long feared; the rain forest is vanishing faster than ever. The 1990s alone were a horrible decade for the Amazon. That decade, destruction of the rainforest reached record levels. In 1995 alone, people burned or cleared more than 11,000 acres of trees—nearly twice what they had destroyed the year before. So far, roughly one-eighth of the rain forest has been destroyed, and it is never coming back.

Deciding to Act

With this bad news comes some good news. Alarmed by these statistics, the people of Brazil pledged to do a better job of protecting the rain forest. First, they promised to do a better job of enforcing their laws. They had finally realized they were at risk of losing a national treasure, and they were finally ready to do something about it.

To honor its pledge, in 1996 Brazil got tougher on people who abused the rain forest. It limited the amount of land people could clear. Initially, it seemed Brazil's efforts were working. In 1997, destruction of the rain forest slowed. Some argued that this progress wasn't due to the government's efforts at all, though. They said it had just been more difficult to cut trees that year because it had rained more than usual. Whatever the reason, there have been other challenges created by Brazil's government. Sadly, country officials didn't always enforce the laws.

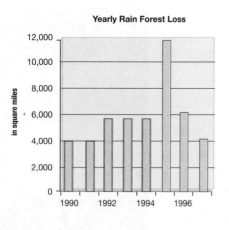

Now, though, Brazil is getting tough again. The government has promised to punish people who abuse the rain forest. They'll give them stiff fines and force them to fix their damage. With luck, these new efforts will have a lasting impact. Sadly, the Amazon is still at risk of extinction. It is far from being "out of the woods" yet.

Editorial Assistance by Brian McNab

If you were taking notes, what would you have so far? Circle some important information.

How does the accompanying chart illustrate what you read here?

If you had to write a sub-heading here, what would it be?

Does this last piece of information give you a clue about what kind of writing this is?

Reread the passage, and ask yourself the questions in the margin again. Then, do Numbers 1 through 6.

1 What feature of this passage would be found in a newspaper or magazine article?

   A   a sub-heading

   B   editorial line at the end of the passage

   C   a chart to illustrate information in the passage

   D   a title

2 According to the graph, the least amount of damage occurred in the rain forest in

   F   1991

   G   1994

   H   1995

   J   1996

3 On the lines below, write a few notes you might take on this passage.

_____

_____

_____

NOTICE: Photocopying any part of this book is forbidden by law.

141

4 Which of the following would be a good sub-heading for the last paragraph?

  A "Getting Tough—and Staying Tough"

  B "Brazil—A Great Place to Visit"

  C "How to Build a Forest Fire"

  D "The Animals of the Amazon"

5 In this passage, it would be important to note

  F Piranhas in Brazil are considered fierce.

  G In 1995, destruction of the rain forest reached record levels.

  H Parrots in the Amazon are brightly colored.

  J Brazil has government officials.

6 How would this passage be different if it were written for a textbook? Write your answer on the lines below.

_____

_____

_____

Discuss your answer with your teacher or class

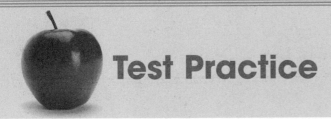

Test Practice

Look at the following chart. Then do Numbers 1 and 2.

Our Office

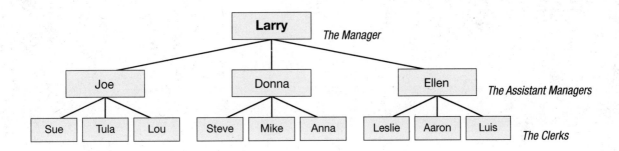

1 This chart illustrates

   A how an organization is set up

   B the cause and effect of working

   C how to get ahead in the workplace

   D where to find an office

2 According to this chart, who does Aaron report directly to?

   F Luis

   G Joe

   H Larry

   J Ellen

Read the following passage about glaciers. Then do Number 3.

Glaciology is the study of glaciers. Glaciers are giant, slow-moving masses of ice that form on land. The study of glaciers also covers the general study of ice.

Glaciology doesn't focus only on ice on earth. Glaciologists, the people who study glaciers, also look for evidence of ice and water elsewhere. Recently, they've looked in places like Mars and Europa, a moon of Jupiter. Spacecraft have detected signs of ice on Europa. By looking at the landscape, they can detect signs of water and ice, such as landforms that appear to have once been riverbeds or valleys.

As scientists learn more about Earth and the planets beyond it, glaciology will be an important science for generations to come.

3 Which notes would you take after reading this passage? Write your answer on the lines below.

> **Read the following passage about monarch butterflies. Then do Numbers 4 and 5.**

No one could believe it, but there they were—a huge flock of more than 25,000 monarch butterflies in one spot!

In fall 1999, the butterflies descended on the town of Cape May, New Jersey. "It really was a sight to see," said Betty Mondale. "It was like a huge, fluttering, brightly-colored cloud!"

According to Karen Oberhauser of the University of Minnesota, the fair weather that year helped the butterflies. There had been plenty of rain, which had helped the milkweed plants grow, and monarch butterflies love milkweed.

Milkweed plants play a role in the lifecycle of the monarch. The butterflies sleep all winter long in the south. In the spring, they awaken and start to fly north. As they do, the females each lay up to 7,000 eggs on the undersides of milkweeds. After that, sadly, they die.

The eggs they laid, though, grow into striped caterpillars in about a month. Those caterpillars grow into adult butterflies. Each generation of butterflies lives about two months. The cycle starts again when the females lay more eggs.

The future of the monarch is in doubt. Many forests where the butterflies spend the winter have been destroyed. Farmers use weed killers that destroy milkweed. Others, though, know the monarchs are survivors. "They aren't just beautiful," said Mondale. "They're strong."

4 What would be a good title for this passage?

   A "Who Needs Milkweed?"

   B "Too Many Caterpillars"

   C "Winter in the South"

   D "It's Raining Monarchs!"

5 How would you rewrite this passage for a textbook? Be sure to include suggestions for headings, sub-headings, and illustrations.

_____

_____

_____

_____

_____

_____

_____

_____

_____

_____

_____

_____

_____

_____

_____

_____

CHAPTER 5

Fine Points of Reading

Lesson 16: Understanding Format

The way text is organized affects how you understand it. Being able to find the information you want or need is as important as having it. Suppose you're asked to write a report on the Brooklyn Dodgers. Which of these books would you read?

> *New York Landmarks*
> *Sports Teams in America*
> *How to Play Baseball*
> *The Principles of Good Sportsmanship*

You'd probably use the second book, *Sports Teams in America*. Why? Because its title tells you that it contains information about sports teams like the Brooklyn Dodgers. The first book wouldn't help you, because the Dodgers aren't a New York landmark. While the Dodgers played baseball, the third book is about how to play the game in general, not how the Dodgers played it. As far as the last book goes, good sportsmanship is important to baseball, but a book like this won't give you the right information.

A book's **title**, which tells you the book's general topic, appears on the cover of the book and on the title page. The title page usually includes information like the names of the illustrator or editor (if there is one) and the publisher.

Read the passage below, and then answer the question that follows.

Andersen's Fairy Tales
Illustrated by Maxwell Armfield
Children's Classics: New York

Describe the kind of stories you would expect to find in a book with this title. Would they be realistic or imaginative? Be as specific as possible.

_____

_____

_____

_____

_____

_____

_____

_____

 What kind of information do fairy tales include? Is this information considered fiction or nonfiction?

Example 1

Rivers: One Way to Avoid Traffic

Holland: A Great Place to Visit

Great Waterways in New York

About New York Architecture

1 **Which of these books would you use to find information about the Holland Tunnel in New York?**

A *Rivers: One Way to Avoid Traffic*

B *Holland: A Great Place to Visit*

C *Great Waterways in New York*

D *About New York Architecture*

The Holland Tunnel is a structure in New York.

Titles and title pages are just some of the tools authors use to organize information so you can easily find it. Another tool that makes your search easier is a table of contents, especially if you're looking for information in a textbook.

A **table of contents** provides more detailed information than the title. It lists the chapters in the book, as well as the pages those chapters start on. You can find the table of contents at the beginning of a book.

Example 2

Chapter 1:	The History of Dairy Farming in New York	p. 1
Chapter 2:	How to Milk a Dairy Cow	p. 7
Chapter 3:	Other Jobs on the Dairy Farm	p. 17
Chapter 4:	Finding Dairy Farms in New York	p. 23

2a **This passage is an example of a**

A   poem

B   chapter title

C   table of contents

D   book title

This passage contains the titles of chapters and the pages where the chapters start.

2b **Which page would you look on to find where dairy farms are located in New York?**

F   1

G   7

H   17

J   23

One of these chapters tells how to find dairy farms in New York.

Another tool authors use to help you find information is the index. The **index** lists all kinds of subjects from the book, as well as the page numbers where you can find them. To make finding the subject you want easier, the index lists subjects in alphabetical order. Usually, you find the index at the back of a book.

Example 3

Abbott, George   18, 27, 233
Akwesasne   42, 88
Albany Pine Bush Reserve   59, 84
Apple picking   3, 19, 47

3a **This passage is an example of**

A   a chapter

B   an index

C   a table of contents

D   a title

The items are in alphabetical order.

3b **Which of these pages would you look on to find information about George Abbott?**

F   3

G   19

H   27

J   88

Discuss your answer with your teacher or class.

Standard: S1.I.1.F Understand and use the text features that make information accessible and usable, such as format, sequence, level of diction, and relevance of details.

Lesson 17
Understanding Sequence

An argument is a disagreement between two or more people who are talking. In a piece of writing, an **argument** is the position an author takes either for or against a particular subject.

Sometimes, the author's argument is clear. For example, when people write letters to their state or local representatives, they usually state their issues and then their positions on those issues. Consider the following example:

Dear Representative Carney:

    There has recently been a lot of discussion about whether or not to build a new dock on Oneida Lake. We're in favor of building the dock.

Here, the authors first state their issue: Should a dock be built on Oneida Lake? Then they go on to explain that they support the dock.

So now what? Is the argument over? Actually, no. The authors have just gotten started. The next step is to explain why they've taken their position. Without that kind of an explanation, an argument isn't very strong. A good argument has two parts:

- what the author wants the reader to think or do
- the reasons the author wants the reader to think or do that

Read the passage below, and then answer the question that follows.

I really like New York apples. They're my favorite food. I eat them all the time. I'd eat them for every meal if I could. Everybody should eat apples, but only the ones from New York. They're better than the apples from anywhere else.

Has the author made a good argument? If not, explain how you might make it better.

_____

_____

_____

 HINT A good argument not only raises a topic, it tells you what you should think or feel—and why.

People who make arguments usually feel very strongly about them, so it's important to build arguments well.

Let's continue with our dock example. We already know that the authors want their local representative to build a new dock on Oneida Lake. So the next step is to tell the representative why.

In an argument, certain kinds of reasons work well. A really good argument addresses the reader's concerns. This means the authors give reasons for their position and also respond to whatever objections they think their readers might have. Does that sound complicated? It's really not.

Let's say we're arguing in favor of the Oneida Lake dock. What reasons could we have? Not all reasons are equally convincing. For instance, you might want the dock because you live on Oneida Lake and your neighbors at another lake have one, but that won't convince anyone. What about the fact that the new dock will make boating on Oneida Lake safer? That would be more convincing because a lot of readers probably worry about safety.

To find convincing reasons for an argument, think about the topic in general. What makes a dock on a lake a good idea? As we just mentioned, docks can improve boating safety. With a new dock, boats will have a safe place to stay. Docks can improve entertainment. You and your family could have a new place to swim. Docks can even improve the local economy. People would be needed to build the dock, which would mean more jobs would be created.

Example 1

Morning is the best time to exercise. Studies have shown that people who exercise in the morning are more likely to stick with their exercise routines. Morning exercise boosts the metabolism for the whole day. Also, if you shower after your morning exercise, you won't need to shower for the rest of the day.

1a **The author is trying to convince you to**

   A exercise so you can eat more

   B shower twice a day

   C exercise in the morning

   D boost your metabolism

 Think about the main point the author argues.

1b **What is one reason the author gives to support the argument?**

   F Morning exercise boosts the metabolism.

   G There are studies on exercise.

   H Morning is the best time to exercise.

   J People exercise in the morning.

 Only one of these choices could convince a reader to support the author's argument.

While the reasons for doing or thinking something—positive arguments—are usually the most convincing when making an argument, you can also point out the effects of not doing or thinking something. These are called negative arguments. If you were arguing in favor of building a new dock on Oneida Lake, for example, you could use the negative argument that not building the dock would hurt the local economy. Try not to spend too much time on the negative. Doing so focuses your reader's attention in the wrong place.

When you're forming an argument, what you're trying to do is convince your reader to feel the way you do. Hard evidence—like studies and statistics—may convince your readers that your position is the right one. They may agree intellectually that it makes sense, but that may not be enough to convince them. If you make your readers care about your issue by appealing to their emotions, you'll likely convince them. Only then will your argument be very strong.

Example 2

Coyotes would be an inspiring mascot for our new school. Like us, who almost saw our school closed down, coyotes are survivors. In the Mohawk Valley school district, we always pull together, and so do coyotes. They work in packs, and their all-for-one, one-for-all attitude inspires our sports teams to even greater achievement, and so will the howls of support from Mohawk Valley's ever-devoted fans.

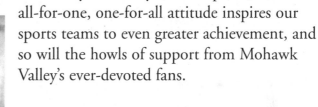

2 **What emotion does the author <u>not</u> appeal to?**

   A   pride

   B   desire to win

   C   sense of independence

   D   school spirit

SELF
Coach™   Discuss your answer with your teacher or class.

Standard: S1.I.1.F Understand and use the text features that make information accessible and usable, such as format, sequence, level of diction, and relevance of details.

Lesson 18
Understanding Diction

We all have a way of speaking. Most of us learn how to speak from our parents, our teachers, and our friends. We often tend to speak as they do. **Diction** is made up of the words we say, how we use them, even how we say them. In writing, diction is the set of words the author uses to tell a story, write a poem, or bring characters to life.

Some diction makes the writing more believable. The words an author chooses affect readers. For example, how could an author describe a basic rock formation? As a "stone," a "boulder," or an "outcropping." What about a "pile of rocks"? A "mound"? If the author wanted to get really fancy, he or she could call that pile of rocks a "geological feature." The reader might think differently about that rock formation—and the writer! Good writers think about how audiences will react to different words.

 THINKING IT THROUGH Read the passage below, and then answer the question that follows.

"That is absolutely, undeniably <u>not</u> what occurred," the young woman said crisply. "I deny the charges, and I want the record to show that I am gravely disappointed."

Who might this passage be written for? Give examples to support your response.

_____

_____

_____

_____

HINT! Think about the kinds of words the author uses.

Writing that uses very elaborate or very technical vocabulary—words with lots of syllables—is considered "high" or "formal" diction. Authors may use this kind of diction to imply that a character is smart, sophisticated, or highly educated. In contrast, authors use very simple words, even slang, to suggest that their characters are down-to-earth.

Example 1

Read this passage and answer the question that follows.

Itchin' to visit New York's Finger Lakes? Dyin' to get outside again? Can you already smell the fresh air and feel the earth beneath your feet?

Then wait no more! Come on over to glorious, sun-kissed, wide-open upstate New York! Whatever the season, we've got something fun for you! In the winter, bundle up, 'cause we've got skiing, sledding, snowshoeing, and ice skating, too! If you prefer the warm weather, come join us for camping and hiking!

1a **Which of the following is an example of more friendly, down-to-earth diction?**

A "Whatever the season, we've got something fun for you!"

B "Itchin' to visit New York's Finger Lakes?"

C "Come join us for camping and hiking!"

D "Then wait no more."

The author uses casual language to appeal to the readers.

1b **The author uses diction to appeal to readers who are**

F outdoorsy

G warm

H cold

J strict

Discuss your answer with your teacher or class.

Standard: S1.I.1.F   Understand and use the text features that make information accessible and usable, such as format, sequence, level of diction, and relevance of details.

Coached Reading

The following passage is about the debate over a city's budget. As you read the passage and accompanying budget report material, use the statements and questions in the margin to help your understanding.

 Your teacher may read this selection to you.

It's that time of year again. It's time for the city to do its budget, but, once again, there appears to be a serious problem: we have too little money. To solve this problem, Mayor Goldie Schneider has suggested we increase taxes. She thinks we can use the extra money to fix the budget. "I care not one bit what the people think," she once sniffed. "They do not run this city—I do. So I will simply ask for more taxes!"

Members of the City Council, though, disagree with the mayor. They think the best way to fix the budget is to cut things back. They want to cut things like services. They argue, for example, that we can run fewer buses and have fewer summer programs. If we truly want to fix this problem once and for all, the best thing we can do is leave taxes like they are and reduce city services to a more reasonable level.

Eighty percent of the city budget is being used for things that don't benefit city residents, and that's not right. People work hard for their money, and we should use it. A city's budget should help the city's people. Right now, the budget is paying for the mayor's car, and that's just plain wrong. "I will not live like a lowly pauper," the mayor cried when I confronted her about it. "I want my Rolls Royce, and I shall have it!"

> Do you get a sense of how the mayor speaks? Does she seem proper or casual?

> What does the narrator of this passage want to happen?

> What kinds of words does the mayor use? What about the narrator? Circle one or two examples.

> Does the narrator give a reason for the argument? What is it?

We can reduce services and save money without hurting the city's people. For example, if we reduce spending by ten percent in all the city's departments, we can still provide most services. Those departments will simply have to be more efficient and spend money more wisely. They can shop for the equipment and supplies that have the best prices, for example.

We also need to avoid raising taxes in this city. The average person pays $8,000 a year in taxes. That's outrageous. If we increase taxes on top of that, most people won't be able to afford to live here anymore. This city is their home. We can't let them leave.

> How does the narrator support the argument here?

If the mayor gets her way and raises taxes, she's actually making the problem worse, not better. If she raises taxes and people are forced to leave, there will be fewer people here, and that's fewer people to pay taxes. If that happens, we'll have even less money in the budget. That doesn't solve anything.

> Does the narrator give another reason in favor of the argument? What is it?

The people of this city are hardworking and honest. They work hard to pay their taxes, and they deserve to have their money spent wisely. The people we trust to prepare the budget and deliver city services should do just that. By making poor financial decisions, city leaders are letting down the very people who elected them to office.

> How does the narrator's diction help support the argument?

Mayor Schneider needs to show that she respects the residents of this city. She needs to do the right thing, which is to avoid raising taxes and reduce the cost of public services— slightly. Read through her proposal. I've put its table of contents below, so you can get a glance at it. When you do, we hope you'll join our fight.

Mayor Schneider's Budget Proposal

Reread the passage, and ask yourself the questions in the margin again. Then do Numbers 1 through 6.

1 The title of the proposal is

A "Tax Increase Proposal"

B "Budget for Education"

C "Budget Overview"

D "Mayor Schneider's Budget Proposal"

2 It is likely you would find tax information in the chapter called

F "Budget Overview"

G "Tax Increase Proposal"

H "Budget for Services"

J "Budget for Transportation"

3 How does the narrator support the argument? Write your answer on the lines below.

_____

_____

_____

_____

_____

_____

4 In which chapter would you find information on the City Council?

A 1

B 3

C 15

D 33

5 What reason does the mayor give for raising taxes?

F She works hard.

G She pays taxes.

H She runs the city.

J She wants to keep her lifestyle.

6 How do the word choices of the mayor and the narrator differ? Write your answer on the lines below.

_____

_____

_____

_____

_____

_____

Test Practice

Read the following text from a book. Then do Numbers 1 and 2.

Children's Treasure Chest

1 Which page should you look on to find information about umbrellas?

A   138

B   151

C   235

D   238

2 It is likely that Chapter 5 will contain

F   nursery rhymes

G   silly poetry

H   stories

J   wishes

> **Read the following passage about recycling. Then do Numbers 3 through 6.**

America's population is growing fast—too fast! At this rate, we won't have nearly enough supplies! We've got to recycle our resources!

When World War II ended and all the soldiers returned home to America, there was what people called a "baby boom." People started to have young'uns. Lots of them. As a result, we needed more houses, more schools. America started producing a whole lot more—more food, more jobs, just more all around. How do you figure we were doing all that? We needed resources.

I was still just a pup when people began to see that if we kept using things up, soon we'd be out of supplies. That got people's attention. Their little ones wouldn't have anything to eat. It took folks a while to realize that our forests would be gone and our dumps would take over our cities.

So what did I do? I started what I like to call the "conservation movement." It's just a fancy way to say we've got to dig in and reuse and recycle materials whenever possible. Instead of using too much of something, just take what you need. Instead of just tossing things out, rinse them out and use them again. If we all do our part and pitch in by reusing materials and using only what we need, we'll have enough for everybody. The future of this great country of ours depends on it.

3 The author says "We've got to dig in and reuse" to show that

A we've got to focus on recycling

B remember who does and does not recycle

C look for places to find recyclables

D we've got to think about ourselves

4 Which of the following does not support the author's argument?

F The forests will be gone.

G People won't have enough food.

H People fought in World War II.

J Landfills will overrun the city.

5 In this passage the author argues that

A people shouldn't go to war

B kittens shouldn't play with porcupines

C babies need more baths

D there aren't enough resources

164

6 What does the style and wording of this passage tell you about the author? How would different word choices, style, and order change the author's diction? Use specific examples to support your response.

_____

_____

_____

_____

_____

_____

_____

_____

_____

_____

_____

_____

_____

_____

_____

_____

_____

_____

_____

_____

Standard: S1.I.1.F Understand and use the text features that make information accessible and usable, such as format, sequence, level of diction, and relevance of details.

Lesson 19
Context Clues

Sometimes when you're reading, you come across a word you don't know. So what do you do? Do you find a dictionary, look the word up, and then go back to reading? You could, but that would slow you down and distract you. And what do you do if you see a word you don't know on a test? Are you stuck?

There's a way to figure out the meanings of words on your own, and that's called **context**. Context refers to the other words and sentences in a piece of writing. They give meaning to the rest of the writing. By considering a word's context, you can often figure out what that word means. Look at the following sentence:

> I usually have an apple with lunch, but today I decided to try a kiwi.

If you don't know what a kiwi is, you can still figure out its meaning by reading the rest of the sentence and checking for context. The first part of the sentence, "I usually have an apple with lunch" is easy enough to understand. Now look at the second part of the sentence, "but today I decided to try a kiwi." Even without knowing what a kiwi is, you can tell that a kiwi is a kind of food. What, after all, is lunch for? Eating food! This is what it means to use context.

There's another way to approach context. Try reading the sentence again, but this time replace "kiwi" with a blank space.

> I usually have an apple with lunch, but today I decided to try a _____.

Now fill that space with a word or phrase you think would fit. What about an orange or a banana?

Using this approach, you can tell that a kiwi is something else you eat. You might guess it's another type of fruit. You're right. A kiwi is a soft fruit that tastes like a combination of a lemon and a plum. See? Context works.

Now let's use context to figure out the meaning of a verb. Look at the following sentence:

> While Jamar looked for CDs, Martine meandered through the mall, looking in shop windows.

What does the word "meandered" mean? Again, let's look at its context. We can assume Martine and Jamar are in a record store. You can tell this because Jamar is looking for CDs. Meanwhile, Martine "meanders" in the mall. She's moving forward, but she's not going anywhere in particular. She's just "looking in shop windows." So "meandered" is probably another word for "wandered."

Even if you can't pinpoint a word's meaning using context, you can usually get a general enough idea to get you by until you have a chance to look the word up later.

Example 1

"Come on, Kavi," Yoshe said to the grinning boy. "I know you aced the math test, but you can't possibly tell how many grains of sand—or ants—are in our ant farm. You're not omniscient. Sometimes there's things even you can't tell."

1 **Read this sentence from the passage:**

> You're not omniscient. Sometimes there's things even you can't tell.

What does the word *omniscient* mean?

A jealous

B arrogant

C all knowing

D angry

Think about which word fits best in the sentence.

Example 2

By the time we got back to the farm that night, a flock of bluebirds had arrived. Immediately, our day seemed brighter. Just that morning, it had seemed so dark. The innocent little birds were full of life and vivacity. They were so unlike the dark crows that had destroyed our crops. Now we'd have very little food for winter, but the bright coats of the bluebirds, and their uplifting songs made things seem just a little better.

> **2** **Read this sentence from the passage:**
>
> The innocent little birds were full of life and vivacity.
>
> **What does the word *vivacity* mean?"**
>
> **A** seeds
>
> **B** spirit
>
> **C** blue
>
> **D** coat
>
>  Only one of these words completes the sentence in a way that makes sense.

Example 3

At the restaurant, she asked me to place our order in Spanish. Unfortunately, I couldn't oblige. I only know a smattering of the language; certainly not enough to be of much help.

3 The reader can tell that the word "smattering" means "a little" because the

A restaurant was fancy

B woman wanted the order in Spanish

C husband didn't know enough to help

D order was for a Spanish dish

SELF Coach

Discuss your answer with your teacher or class.

Standards: S1.I.1.E. relate new information to prior knowledge and experience
S1.I.1.F. understand and use the text features that make information accessible and usable, such as format, sequence, level of diction, and relevance of details.

Lesson 20
Making Inferences

An **inference** is a decision you make based on information you have. To make an inference, you have to have some kind of evidence. For example, what if you were walking past your school auditorium and you saw people fanning themselves and wiping their foreheads as they left? You wouldn't need to see flames or fire trucks to infer that it was hot inside the auditorium. Your experience and knowledge would tell you all you needed to know.

Basically, an inference is the most likely interpretation of a situation, given the information that's available. In literature, you use the information that's available to you to make inferences about:

- a character's personality, interests, or physical appearance
- a character's history
- a character's age
- the history of relationships between characters
- the reasons for a character's behavior
- a character's intentions
- a character's next action

THINKING IT THROUGH   Read the passage below, and then answer the question that follows.

   Yoshe spied the cupcake on the counter and immediately her mouth began to water. She hadn't eaten all day, and dinner was still several hours away. Thinking just a minute more, she started to move.

What can you infer from this passage? What do you conclude will happen?

_____

_____

_____

HINT   Think about the clues you get about Yoshe's behavior. Given that, what do you think she'll do?

As a student, you'll often be asked to make an inference about a piece of writing—then you'll be asked to support that inference. Supporting your inference means explaining why you inferred what you did. To do this, you need to use specific examples from the piece of writing.

Example 1

Lukas was tall and robust at 200 pounds. When he spoke, he spoke with a deep booming voice and an Eastern European accent. He was also a very outgoing person. It was hard not to notice when he was in the room. He had many friends, and he loved to tell them stories about his homeland.

He cared about one thing even more than friendship, though. He worked toward it every day. Every night after work, in his small apartment, Lukas read his books and listened to his tapes. He was studying business. Someday he would open his own shop, and he would become an important part of the community.

1a Which example is not a way the author implies something about Peter in this passage?

A He spoke a lot.

B He was very tall.

C He had many friends.

D He worked hard afterwork.

Remember that evidence in a passage supports an inference.

1b From this passage, you can infer that Peter

F frightened people with his size

G liked living at the boardinghouse

H confused people with his accent

J had high ambitions

One of these answers can be supported by details from the passage.

When making inferences, always be sure to read a passage carefully. Only then try to determine the proper inference. Each time, read the passage first, then consider all the evidence, and, finally, think about which inferences you can draw given that evidence.

Example 2

Some of you may know Lucille Ball from an old, old TV show. There was a time when she was one of America's favorite comedy stars. Lucille Ball was never a typical comedian, especially at the time she started. She started in comedy back in the 1930s, when funny ladies were only supposed to be funny, and nothing more. They weren't supposed to look or act anything like her.

Lucille was destined for many great things from the beginning. She was born in August 1911, in Jamestown, New York. When she was 15, she entered the John Murray Anderson Drama School in New York City. She tried many times to get into Broadway chorus lines. She only turned to modeling when that didn't work.

Lucille really wanted to act. Modeling wasn't what she wanted to do. Using the name Diane Belmont, she became a successful model. That success led Lucille to her first movie role in 1934. Finally, she was on her way to making her real dream come true.

2 **From this passage, you can infer that Lucille was**

A destined for great things

B beautiful as well as funny

C born in Jamestown, New York

D in the movie *Roman Scandals*

Discuss your answer with your teacher or class.

Standard: S2.I.1.C. Identify significant literary elements (including metaphor, symbolism, foreshadowing, dialect, rhyme, meter, irony, climax) and use those elements to interpret the work.

Lesson 21
Author's Point of View

As you know, every story has a narrator who tells the story. The narrator's point of view is the perspective, or position, from which the story is told. In literature, there are two main points of view: **first person** and **third person**.

Point of View	Definition	Example
First person	Passage told from the personal ("I," "we," or "us") point of view. The narrator is a character in the story.	We went to the baseball game, but I didn't get to see much of it. Travis got to stay, while I had to go home.
Third person	The narrator isn't a character in the story. The pronouns "he," "she," or "it" represent characters.	Martin and Travis went to the baseball game. Travis got to stay, but Martin had to leave early.

Read the passage below, and then answer the question that follows.

I couldn't believe she did that! I mean, we had an agreement! Mom said if I did my homework I could go for a horseback ride, as long as I wore my helmet. So I did my homework, and now she won't let me go! That's just not fair!

Is this story told from first-person or third-person point of view?

_____

_____

_____

 HINT   The narrator uses the word "I."

Example 1

Martine loved to go to the flea market with her mother, and today was the perfect day for it. First of all, it was Saturday. "What better day?" Martine asked herself merrily. "We have all the time in the world." And second? It wasn't too warm. "I like it warm, but not too warm," she thought. "Especially when you're walking around, trying to find treasures."

She settled into the back seat as her mother drove across town, but when the pair reached the market, Martine was too excited to relax any more. As soon as the car stopped, she hopped out, and her mother followed. "Come on Mom, let's find some bargains. You know how much I love to find bargains!"

Soon, mother and daughter were inspecting all the wares in the market's aisles. Martine was savoring a piece of fudge from one of the vendors when something caught her eye. It was too good to be true!

"Look Mom!" she beckoned her mother. Her mother followed her daughter's outstretched hand to the top of a nearby table. There, at the end of Martine's finger, was an antique microscope. "Please Mom, do you think we can get it?" Martine implored. "You know how much I love science. I don't think I can live without it!"

---

1 **This passage is written from which point of view?**

A first person

B second person

C third person

D fourth person

QUICK
Coach

Note that the characters, not the narrator, use words like "I" and "we" in the passage.

Point of view also involves the author or narrator's feelings. Every story has a narrator, and every story has an author, but they're not always the same person.

Authors' points of view reflect what they were thinking when they wrote their stories. They reflect why they wrote their stories. As you read, try to figure out what the authors hope to accomplish with their stories. For example, an author may write a story about how buses are better than the subway in New York City, hoping you'll agree.

Example 2

For years, this city has been declining. Crime is up, jobs are down. People no longer feel safe in the streets. They need a change, a big one. The current administration has been unable to turn things around. This city needs a new captain at its helm, somebody who will steer the city through its financial storm. Who's that person? Jose Portese.

You may know that Jose is running for mayor. But what you may not know is that Jose wants to lower city taxes, bring in new businesses, and increase the number of parking spaces downtown. He also wants to reorganize city departments to save money and improve services to senior citizens. Jose would make a great mayor. Everybody should vote for him.

2 What is the author's point of view in this passage?

A The crime rate is improving.

B The city needs to spend more.

C Jose will improve the city.

D Jose will spend more on making new parking spaces.

Discuss your answer with your teacher or class.

Standards: S1.I.1.E. Relate new information to prior knowledge and experience.

S1.I.1.F. Understand and use the text features that make information accessible and usable, such as format, sequence, level of diction, and relevance of details.

S2.I.1.C. Identify significant literary elements (including metaphor, symbolism, foreshadowing, dialect, rhyme, meter, irony, climax) and use those elements to interpret the work.

Coached Reading

The following passage is about a man who sets out to get a glass of water. As you read the passage, use the statements and questions in the margin to help your understanding.

 Your teacher may read this selection to you.

Getting a Glass of Water

Adapted from the original by Frederick W. Cozzens

One evening, I was busy writing when I decided I wanted a glass of water. I took the candle and a pitcher and went down to the pump in the kitchen.

First, I had to open a bolted door to get into the basement hall, and then I went to the kitchen door, which was locked. Then I remembered that our maid always carried the key to bed with her and slept with it under her pillow. I retraced my steps, bolted the basement door, and went up to the dining room. As is always the case, I found when I could get no water I was thirstier than I'd assumed. Then I thought I would wake our girl up, but I decided not to.

Then I thought of the well outside, but I gave that up on account of its flavor. Then I opened the closet doors; there was no water there. Then I thought of the dumbwaiter in our house. It was useful for carrying trays and laundry from one floor to another. Why couldn't it carry me? The novelty of the idea made me smile. I took the pitcher on the

From what point of view is the narrator telling this story?

What is the author's point of view in this story? Why does he decide not to awaken the girl?

Can you infer anything at this point in the story?

A dumbwaiter is an old-fashioned small elevator. Many houses used to have them.

bottom of the dumbwaiter, got myself in with the lamp, let myself down until a foot away from the floor below, and let go.

It came down so suddenly I shot out of the elevator as if it had been a <u>catapult</u>. It broke the pitcher, extinguished the lamp, and landed me in the middle of the kitchen at midnight. It turns out I wasn't as close to the bottom as I'd thought. I knew I couldn't go back up the way I'd come down, and there was no way I'd be able to force the bolted door open. I thought to go out the window. Then I remembered that I'd put in rigid iron bars to keep people out. For that, I felt a bit angry at myself.

Leaning as far out the open window as I could, I began shouting and banging a kettle to make noise. That only caused the neighbor's dogs to start barking. Then I heard Mrs. Sparrowgrass calling to me from the top of the staircase. I shouted back to her, but the dogs' barking drowned out my voice. When she couldn't get me to respond, she became frightened and summoned the neighbor, who came to the rescue with a lantern and a massive bull-terrier. Great. Another one. But this one was supposed to know me! The moment the creature saw me at the window, he, too, began to growl. I threw myself under the kitchen table and tried to reason with him, but he would not listen. In the excitement I had forgotten his name, and that made matters worse. Finally, the creature's owner woke everybody up, broke down the basement door with an axe, and got into the kitchen. Then the creature recognized me. His owner then wanted me to explain myself, but what could I say?

What about this point of the story? Can you infer the kinds of things that will happen?

Are there any words in this story you do not know? Circle any words you may need context for.

Can you infer the kind of story the author intended to write? What kinds of things happen to the narrator, and why?

NOTICE: Photocopying any part of this book is forbidden by law.

179

Reread the passage, and ask yourself the questions in the margin again. Then, do Numbers 1 through 6.

1 In this passage, the word "catapult" means

A something that flips people or objects forward

B a small elevator

C a large, angry dog

D a kind of well

2 What can you conclude about the narrator?

F He could see well in the dark.

G He liked most kinds of dogs.

H He didn't like to ask for help.

J He usually drank water at night.

3 What is the author's point of view on his experiences in the story? Write your answer on the lines below.

_____

_____

_____

4 **How can you tell what kind of creature a bull-terrier is?**

   A   It growls at the narrator.

   B   It comes with the narrator's neighbor.

   C   The narrator calls it "another one" after mentioning dogs.

   D   The narrator thinks it is supposed to know him.

5 **This passage is told from**

   F   first person point of view

   G   second person point of view

   H   third person point of view

   J   fourth person point of view

6 **Why can you infer early in the story the kinds of things that will happen? Write your answer on the lines below.**

_____

_____

_____

Discuss your answer with your teacher or class

Test Practice

> **Read the following passage about a man and his daughter. Then do Numbers 1 through 3.**

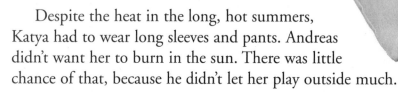

From the time she was little, Andreas took every precaution for his daughter, Katya. He wasn't about to let her get hurt. To keep her from falling out of bed, he had her sleep on the floor. To make her more comfortable there, he lined the mattress with down pillows.

Despite the heat in the long, hot summers, Katya had to wear long sleeves and pants. Andreas didn't want her to burn in the sun. There was little chance of that, because he didn't let her play outside much.

Most of her time Katya spent practicing her violin. She was a sad little girl, feeling lonely and trapped. With her father acting as such a bulwark between her and the world, she had little fun and few friends.

1 What does the word "bulwark" mean?

   A sun worshipper

   B violinist

   C protector

   D bed maker

2 The reader can tell this passage is told from the third-person point of view because

   F the narrator is a character in the story

   G the reader learns nothing about the story

   H the narrator is not part of the story

   J the reader learns nothing about the characters

3 What can you infer from this passage? What can you conclude about Andreas? Explain how this passage would be different if Andreas were not as cautious.

_____

_____

_____

_____

_____

_____

_____

_____

_____

_____

_____

_____

_____

_____

_____

_____

_____

_____

_____

_____

_____

_____

_____

Read the following passage about Goldilocks and the three bears. Then do Numbers 4 through 6.

Goldilocks and the Three Bears

Once upon a time, there was a little girl named Goldilocks. One day, she set out for a walk in the forest. Soon, she happened upon a house. She knocked, and when no one answered, walked right in.

At the table in the kitchen were three bowls of porridge. Goldilocks was famished. It had been hours since breakfast, and she'd been walking for hours. She tasted the porridge from the first bowl. "This porridge is too hot!" she exclaimed. So she tasted the porridge from the second bowl. "And this porridge is too cold." she said. Then she tasted the last bowl of porridge. "Ahhh," she sighed, "this porridge is just right." Happily, she devoured it.

After she'd eaten, she felt a little tired. So she walked into the living room. She saw three chairs. She sat in the first one to rest her feet. "This chair is too big!" she shouted. So she sat in the second one. "This chair is too big, too!" she whined. Finally, she tried the last and smallest chair. "Ahhh," she sighed. "This chair is just right." Just then, the chair broke into pieces.

Goldilocks was very tired by this time, so she went upstairs, where she found a bedroom. In the room were three beds. She lay down in the first bed, but it was too hard. Then she lay in the second bed, but it was too soft. Then she lay down in the third bed, and it was just right. Goldilocks fell right asleep.

As she was sleeping, the three bears came home. "Someone's been eating my porridge," growled Papa Bear. "Someone's been eating my porridge," said Mama Bear. "Someone's been eating my porridge, and they ate it all up!" cried Baby Bear.

"Someone's been sitting in my chair," growled Papa Bear. "Someone's been sitting in my chair," said Mama Bear. "Someone's been sitting in my chair, and they've broken it all to pieces," cried Baby Bear.

Given what had happened, the bears decided to look around some more. When they got upstairs to the bedroom, Papa Bear growled, "Someone's been sleeping in my bed." "Someone's been sleeping in my bed, too," said Mama Bear. "Someone's been sleeping in my bed, and she's still there!" exclaimed Baby Bear.

Just then, Goldilocks awoke and saw the three bears. She screamed loudly and ran from the room. Down the stairs, out the door, and into the forest she ran, and she never returned.

4 This passage is told from which point of view?

    A first person

    B second person

    C third person

    D fourth person

5 In this passage, what does the word "famished" mean?

    F greedy

    G lonely

    H angry

    J hungry

6 What can you conclude about Goldilocks? Use two or three examples.

_____

_____

_____

Standard: S1.I.1.D Distinguish between relevant and irrelevant information and between fact and opinion.

Lesson 22
Essential vs. Nonessential Information

When you're writing a story, or arguing a point, it's important to stay on track. That means including all the information you need to tell your story or make your point. To avoid distracting your readers, leave out unneeded or nonessential information. **Essential information** connects directly to your story or point. **Nonessential information** is not important to the story. Read the following ad:

> Okay, folks—you've given us a running start, and now we're open! Come to us for all your sporting-goods needs, whether you play team sports—like basketball and baseball—or like to spend time camping, fishing, inline skating, and more! We have all you need!
>
> And we've secured the very best spot: in the Lincoln Shopping Plaza, right between Mac's Diner—for the best burgers around—and Zac's Game Stop. Where else would you go for your video games and DVDs? So don't walk—run—to our grand opening!

As you read this ad, what do you notice is missing? Here's a hint: If you were going to this opening, where would you be going? The author of this passage has left out some essential information. The name of the sporting-goods store is the most important thing. Does the reader really need to know that Mac's Diner has the best burgers? This kind of information is considered nonessential. Look at this new version of that ad.

> Okay, folks. You've given us a running start, and now McDougal's Sporting Goods store is finally open! Come to our grand opening this Friday, March 7, from 9 AM until 11 PM at Lincoln Plaza, 7 Salisbury Street. We're conveniently located between Mac's Diner and Zac's Game Stop.
>
> So whether you're in the market for new cleats or some camping gear, walk—don't run—to McDougal's! Our grand opening lasts only one day!

This ad is much better. It has its essential information—the store's name and location and the time of the grand opening—and it's missing the nonessential information about Mac's and Zac's.

Read the passage below, and then answer the question that follows.

While the beaver is common in New York, it is admittedly an odd choice for our school's mascot. But that's a choice we want to make, and there's many reasons why.

First, Craden Middle school likes to stand out from the crowd. It makes sense to have a mascot no other school in the state has, and mascots can be so much fun! Second, the beaver is extremely hardworking, just like we are. We think the beaver is a really good symbol.

Which information is essential to this passage? Which is nonessential?

_____

_____

_____

 Nonessential information does not relate directly to the rest of a passage.

Example 1

In 1492, Christopher Columbus set sail on the Atlantic Ocean. He was about to change sea travel. He was headed west, looking for a new trade route. Instead, he ended up just off the coast of what is now North America. North America was a huge continent. Before Christopher's trip, people avoided long trips over the ocean. They believed many myths about sea travel. Some believed that travelers could fall off the edge of the Earth if they went too far. Others believed in sea serpents and mermaids. As explorers took more chances, and sailed farther, people believed these tales less and less.

1 **The information that is nonessential to this passage is that**

   A Christopher sailed on the Atlantic Ocean.

   B People used to avoid long sea journeys.

   C North America was a huge continent.

   D People believed myths about sea travel.

 Discuss your answer with your teacher or class.

Lesson 23
Fact and Opinion

As you learned in Lesson 1, nonfiction literature is about true things, things that actually happened. But just because something is nonfiction doesn't mean it contains all facts. Nonfiction passages may also contain opinions.

A **fact** can be proven. It is always true. "New York is a state in America" is a fact, because it can be proven. Just look at a map. An **opinion** is a person's belief. It can't be proven true or false. "New York is the best state on the East Coast" is an opinion, because it's what one person believes. Another person may feel that Delaware is the best state.

To understand how facts and opinions differ, look at the following examples:

Facts	Opinions
Chocolate cake contains milk, eggs, and chocolate.	Chocolate cake makes the best birthday cake.
Manuel is the class president.	Olga would make a better class president than Manuel.

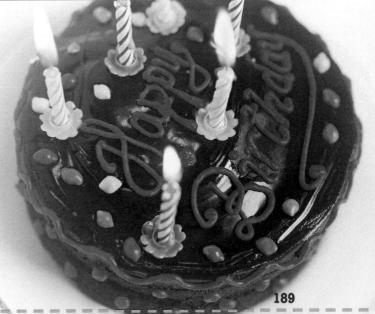

Read the passage below, and then answer the question that follows.

Albany State Assemblywoman Contessa Martin has been in office for four years. For all of those years, she's done a great job. No one could have done it better. She has chaired several committees, including those on transportation and schools, and she succeeded in securing $7 million in funding for her local towns and cities. So when it comes time for reelection, Contessa Martin is the best choice.

What is a fact in this passage? How would you rewrite it to make it an opinion?

_____

_____

_____

 A fact is something you can prove, while an opinion is something someone believes.

When trying to identify opinions, look for words like "best," "always," and "everyone." Look for comparison words like "better." These words are tough to prove, therefore the statements they're in can't be true.

Example 1

The United States and China have very different cultures.

In every culture, members share certain attitudes and beliefs. In American culture, people believe they should live free and succeed or fail based on their skills. The Chinese culture is a little different. It focuses on things like peace and courtesy. Respect is part of Chinese culture.

American culture stresses individual freedom, and many different kinds of people live in the United States successfully. But the Chinese way is better. Why? Because respect is the most important thing in that culture.

China and America define respect differently. To improve relations between the two countries, Americans must work harder to be more like the Chinese.

1a **Which of these sentences from the passage is an opinion?**

A "But the Chinese way is better."

B "Respect is part of Chinese culture."

C "China and America define respect differently."

D "American culture stresses individual freedom. . ."

Remember that an opinion is someone's belief. It cannot be proven true or false.

1b **In this passage, it is a fact that**

F respect is important in Chinese culture

G people in a culture share certain attitudes and beliefs

H Americans must work harder

J Americans should be judged based on respect

Discuss your answer with your teacher or class.

Standard: S1.I.1.E Relate new information to prior knowledge and experience.

Lesson 24
Use Prior Knowledge

Knowledge is an important part of life, especially when you're a student. You use the things you know all the time. When you read books, watch the news, or listen to the radio, you use your knowledge to understand what's being said.

Suppose you live in New York City. What are some things you might know? You might know, for example, that "downtown" means the southern part of Manhattan. And that Brooklyn is a borough. You might even know how to take the subway.

So, when you read a passage about taking the subway in New York City, for example, you can relate the information in the passage to the things you already know. The passage tells you, for instance, that a character is taking a subway instead of a bus. You already know that the subway is underground. Read the following example:

> "Ugh," Mrs. Lightbear's class groaned in unison.
>
> "Not more!" Jamar cried, making the entire class burst into giggles.
>
> "Oh, yes—absolutely more," Mrs. Lightbear replied in a serious tone. "But not much. We have just a few blocks to go to get to the museum. But first, we have to cross the street. Look—there's the crossing guard."

You've probably crossed a street many times. If you've lived in a city, you probably know what a block is. If you live in a city, you probably know that you should use the crosswalk to cross a street. You don't have to live in a city to understand safety. You only know any of these things because you've learned them or experienced them before.

Read the passage below, and then answer the question that follows.

Karen chewed her fingernails impatiently. She was late for work again and her office was all the way across town. She knew there was only one way to get there in time. She didn't like traveling underground, and sometimes there were terrible delays. But there was no other way to get there quickly. It was rush hour and there was a convention in town!

How does what you have experienced affect what you think Karen will do?

_____

_____

_____

 Think about how city people and rural people might assume different things about what Karen is about to do.

We don't all have the same knowledge and experience. Your experience, and the knowledge you got from that experience, changes how you understand new information. When you read something like a flyer for a stereo, for example, you can apply the information you know to understand that information. For instance, you might think the stereo in the flyer is really expensive.

Example 1

From 1892 to 1954, over twelve million people came to the United States from other countries. They came through Ellis Island, a small island in New York Harbor. It's in the upper bay, just off the New Jersey coast. Over the years, Ellis Island has grown. It started at just over three acres, but now it's more than twenty-seven. Most of the excess land came from landfill or dirt from the construction of the New York City subway system.

1 **Given what you know and have learned, you can tell that**

  A   Ellis Island is in New Jersey

  B   people take the subway to Ellis Island

  C   the subways are New York's underground trains

  D   Ellis Island started as a dump

Discuss your answer with your teacher or class.

Coached Reading

The following passage is about mowing lawns in spring. As you read the passage, use the statements and questions in the margin to help your understanding.

Your teacher may read this selection to you.

Finally, the warm weather has again returned. It's been a long, cold, hard winter. With the return of warm weather, the air is once again filled with the sounds of spring—birds chirping, bugs buzzing, children playing. Most of all, the lawnmowers are roaring nonstop. Those machines make the most distinct sound of spring, and they ruin everything.

Of course, it's important to mow your lawn. After all, our local community is known across the state for its impressive green spaces. People here don't simply care about their lawns, they pride themselves on them. The most caring homeowners mow two or three times a week, but that's ridiculous. Some people even have contests to see who has the most beautiful lawn. That's pretty silly, too. Our neighbors park their van on their lawn. Once, the father accidentally slid into a tree, and all their groceries slid into the street.

> Is the narrator expressing a fact or an opinion in the first sentence?

> Using what you know, how do competitive people usually act?

> Does this paragraph need all this information? Circle any nonessential information.

> Can this paragraph be proven? Is it made of facts or opinions?

Unfortunately, some take lawn care a bit too far. The people who must be stopped are those who choose to run their yard equipment early in the morning or late at night. They are ruining our community, and making life a nightmare.

Some days in my neighborhood, the lawnmowers and weed whackers are running as early as 6 AM. Other days, they're going as late as midnight. I'm a person who often works late. As a result, I generally don't get to bed until after midnight, which means I often don't wake up until late in the morning. When people use their lawnmowers shortly after dawn, I'm awakened far too early, and then I can't get back to sleep. My mother has the same sleep patterns, too. Then again, she's always been a night owl.

People who go to bed earlier than I do face a similar problem when neighbors do their yard work late at night. When a loud machine is running in the yard next door, falling asleep can be incredibly difficult. In fact, there's nothing more difficult than trying to fall asleep with noise.

It's also important to note that these machines are also much louder than they should be. If people oiled engines regularly and maintained them correctly, there would be much less noise. Unfortunately, this is not the case.

Clearly, there's only one solution to this problem, and that's a "noise curfew." I would like to make it illegal to operate loud equipment before 9 AM during weekdays, before 10 AM on weekends, and after 9 PM on any night. Those who break the law should be cited and forced to pay a fine. I believe that the law and the fines will stop most people from running their lawnmowers when they shouldn't. The laws will also encourage them to keep the machines running more quietly.

In your experience, can equipment be loud enough to be distracting? Do you know anyone who works late?

What is the narrator expressing here—fact or opinion?

What does your experience tell you about taking care of things? What is usually the result? Does the narrator have a point?

Knowing what you do about laws, what do you think this means? Do you think this will work?

Reread the passage, and ask yourself the questions in the margin again. Then do Numbers 1 through 6.

1 In this passage, it is nonessential information for the reader to know that the

A people mow their lawns late at night

B people mow their lawns early in the morning

C narrator's mother is a night owl

D lawnmowers are loud

2 Which of the following is a fact?

F Lawnmowers make life a nightmare.

G Spring brings warm weather.

H Lawnmowers make the most distinct spring sound.

J People take lawn care too far.

3 When people get competitive, how do they act? Write your answer on the lines below.

_____

_____

_____

NOTICE: Photocopying any part of this book is forbidden by law.

197

4 **Why does the narrator's problem with lawn mowing keep happening?**

   A   The narrator works later in spring.

   B   It's easier to hear things in spring.

   C   People get more competitive in the spring.

   D   People start mowing their lawns every spring.

5 **Why is it essential information that the narrator works late?**

   F   He is a night owl like his mother.

   G   He can't sleep late because people mow early.

   H   He can't get any other shift at work.

   J   He wants to be able to mow his lawn early.

6 **Where in the passage does the author express an opinion? How would you rewrite it to make it a fact? Write your answer on the lines below.**

_____

_____

_____

Discuss your answer with your teacher or class.

Test Practice

Read the following passage about high-speed trains. Then do Numbers 1 through 3.

High-speed trains have different names in different countries. In France, they're called TGVs, which stands for "trains à grande vitesse." That's French for "trains with great speed." In England, they're called HSR, which stands for "high-speed rail." In Japan, they're called "shinkansen," or "bullet trains." Japan has been a technologically advanced country for many years. The bullet train was introduced in 1964. The bullet train is the best mode of transportation.

The bullet train was the world's first high-speed electric train, and it went as fast as 125 miles per hour. The world record for an electric train was set by a TGV in 1981. It got up to 236 miles per hour, but that was unusually fast. TGVs in service today regularly reach a high speed of 186 miles per hour.

1 Which of the following is the author's opinion?

 A The bullet train is the best mode of transportation.

 B TGVs today reach 186 miles per hour.

 C The bullet train was the first high-speed electric train.

 D A TGV set a world speed record.

2 In this passage, it is nonessential information that

 F High-speed trains are called TGVs in France.

 G Japan has been technologically advanced for many years.

 H England calls its high-speed train HSR.

 J The fastest train reached 236 miles per hour.

3 How does what you know affect how you understand this passage? What if you knew more about trains? Less? Explain each, using examples to support your response.

_____

_____

_____

_____

_____

_____

_____

_____

_____

_____

_____

_____

_____

_____

_____

_____

_____

_____

Read the following passage about pearls. Then do Numbers 4 through 6.

Pearls are the most beautiful stones on Earth, and they are made by living creatures. They form inside the shells of oysters and other shellfish. Pearls are not like diamonds. Sometimes, a grain of sand or a tiny stone slips into the oyster's shell. If the oyster can't get it out, it coats the object with shiny fluid called nacre [NAY-ker]. Nacre sounds scary, like a disease! A pearl forms as layers of nacre build up over time. Like snowflakes, no two pearls look exactly alike. The differences are what make pearls so beautiful. Things are more beautiful when they're not perfect.

Originally, people dove for pearls. Divers hauled in boatloads of oysters and opened each one to search for the stone. Not every oyster forms a pearl, though, and not every pearl is round or clear. Even when pearl farmers put objects into oyster shells, only a few make pearls. Pearl farming is a tough trade. Dairy farming is another kind of farming business. Pearl farming, though, is the toughest kind around.

Legend has it that wealthy Roman women wore pearls to bed. When the women woke in the morning, they immediately remembered they were rich. There's another legend about jade. Today, one beautiful pearl remains a luxury.

4 Using what you know, you can tell that pearls

    A form underwater

    B are decreasing in number

    C smell like vanilla

    D can be eaten

5 Which of the following is essential information in the passage?

    F Dairy farming is another kind of farming business.

    G There's another legend about jade.

    H Pearls form inside the shells of oysters.

    J Diamonds form differently than pearls.

6 What is the author's opinion of pearls?

_____

_____

_____

_____

_____

_____

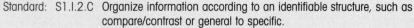

Part 2: Putting it to Use

CHAPTER 6

Organizing Writing

Lesson 25: Compare/Contrast Structure

Comparing things is something we do naturally. It helps make sense of our world. When we know how things are similar and how they're different, we can start to understand their categories.

Look, for example, at the following paragraphs:

> New York and Los Angeles are two of my favorite cities, which is funny. In some ways they're very similar, and in some ways, they're very different. Both are very large cities. Each has millions of people, and each has skyscrapers, apartment buildings, taxi cabs, and buses. They both even have lots of celebrities.
>
> That's where the similarities end. New York, for example, is on the East Coast. And the East Coast, as you may know, can be very cold. Los Angeles, in contrast, is on the West Coast. Unlike in New York, the weather there is usually pretty warm. Many people in New York commute by subway. In Los Angeles, many drive on the freeway.

What are some things you notice right away? You notice how these two cities are similar. And you notice how they're different.

Diagrams are another way to compare and contrast things. Look at this diagram, for instance:

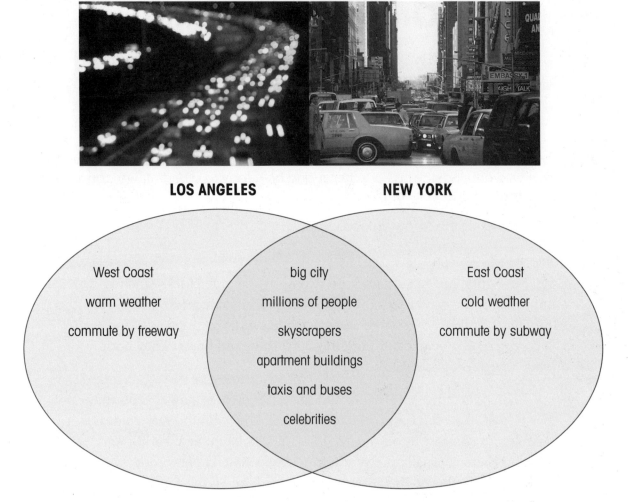

Notice how all the similarities of the cities are in the middle, while all the differences are to the left and right.

Read the passage below, and then answer the question that follows.

Railways and canals are two ways to travel. Think about all the things they share. First, they both transport people. In fact, they both transport goods, and run on schedules. People who travel need to get places. This means they need schedules, and they need responsible people in charge. Both railways and canals have conductors you can rely on to get you and your belongings to your destination safely.

While railways and canals have many things in common, they differ in many ways, too. Think about the mediums they use. Trains travel on land, while canals harness the power of water for travel. The basic vehicles they use are different. Railways use train cars. Canals typically use barges, which are long boats.

How would you complete the following diagram? Use the passage above to fill it in.

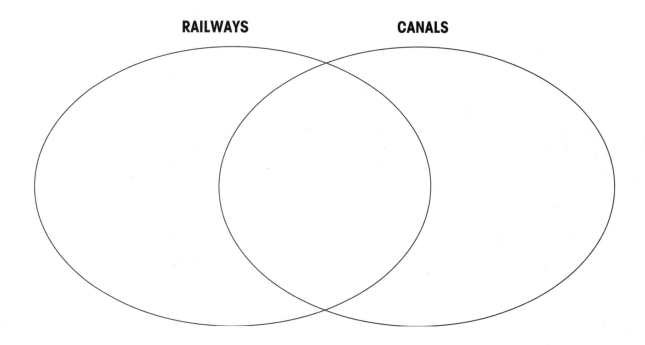

 The center of the diagram should show ways in which railways and canals are similar. Either side of the diagram should show the unique characteristics of each.

Diagrams like these can be very helpful when comparing and contrasting, especially because they're visual. They're also very helpful when you're brainstorming your writing. Why? Because they're a good way to help you organize your thoughts.

Imagine, for example, that you were getting ready to write a passage to compare cross-country and downhill skiing. The first thing you might do is complete a diagram like the one that follows:

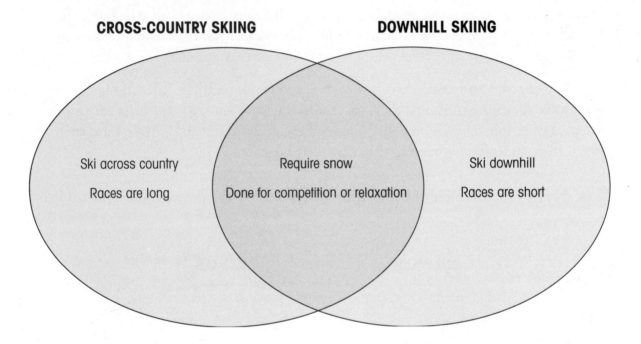

CROSS-COUNTRY SKIING   **DOWNHILL SKIING**

Ski across country

Races are long

Require snow

Done for competition or relaxation

Ski downhill

Races are short

As you brainstormed, you would put all the things you know about the topic on the diagram, making sure to put all the similarities in the middle. As you thought of new things, you could simply add them to the diagram. When you were done, you might get a paragraph like this:

Cross-country or downhill? Both are good. Both require snow, both can help you relax or let you compete. The choice you make, though, depends on the time you have available. Cross-country races are long, going for miles and miles across country. Downhill skiing races, in contrast, are short. You're often down the hill before you know it.

Lesson 26
General to Specific Structure

Comparing and contrasting, as we learned in the last lesson, is one way to organize your thoughts when you're writing. But you can also think about your topic in general, then narrow it until it's specific. When you're unsure about what you want to write about, this can be a good approach.

Think about this as you read the following paragraph:

> Parks can be such treasures—green, lush, and home to so much wildlife. Our nation's parks are the greatest treasures of all, though. They preserve so much of what money can't buy. America has countless parks, but the wide open spaces of the West are prime park space. Take Wyoming, for example. It's home to the oldest national park in the United States: Yellowstone National Park.

As you're reading, what's something you notice about this paragraph? Think about how the paragraph starts—it's very general. By the end, though, it's pretty narrow. By the end it's talking about Yellowstone. Imagine if you were to show this paragraph in a diagram. It might look something like this:

As you can see, the most general topic of the paragraph—parks, is at the top of the pyramid, where the pyramid's widest. It's also at the beginning of the paragraph. Similarly, the most specific item—Yellowstone, is at the point of the pyramid and the end of the paragraph.

Parks

Parks in the United States

Parks in Wyoming

Yellowstone National Park

Example 1

Read the passage below and look at the diagram, and then answer the questions that follow.

In the world of music, there are many legends. There are famous singers, lyricists, and composers. American alone is home to many great composers, some of whom lived in New York. Take George Gershwin, for example. Born in Brooklyn in 1898, he long ago became a music legend, composing classics like "Strike Up the Band" and "Rhapsody in Blue."

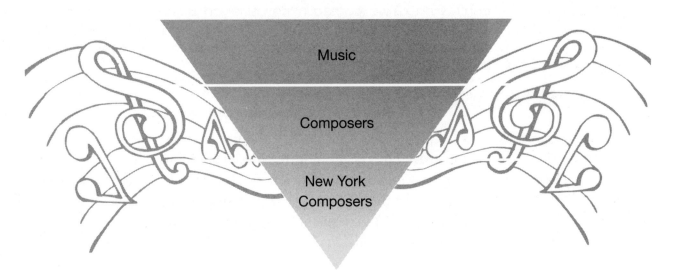

1a The most general piece of information in the passage is

A   Brooklyn

B   George Gershwin

C   music

D   composers

The most general piece of information generally appears at the top of the reversed pyramid and the beginning of a paragraph.

1b Which of the following should go at the bottom of the pyramid?

F   George Gershwin

G   Brooklyn

H   "Strike Up the Band"

J   New York

Discuss your answer with your teacher or class.

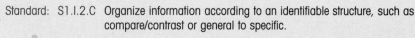

Lesson 27
Main Idea/Details Structure

As you have seen from the last few lessons, most things you read have main ideas and supporting, or specific, information.

The **main idea** is what the writing is mostly about. Newspaper writing, for example, is usually about current events. The main ideas appear in headlines, which you learned about in Chapter 4. A main idea isn't always as obvious as a headline, though. Fiction writers and poets may not state their main ideas. You have to figure them out.

Before you start writing, you should have a main idea in mind. Think about your subject, and then think about how you'll organize your ideas.

As you learned in Chapter 4, charts or graphs can be good ways to illustrate ideas. They can also help you organize your ideas. Think about how you would use graphics to illustrate the following paragraph:

> Most of us don't think about it much, but water, specifically rain, is an essential, vital part of life. Just think about it: rain makes things wet, and the ground needs moisture. Without it, there'd be no water table, and we'd have nothing to drink. Also, water provides essential nutrients to all plant life. Plants are something else we need to survive. Finally, water feeds our rivers and lakes, and those bodies of water are home to other food sources we need, things like fish and aquatic life.

NOTICE: Photocopying any part of this book is forbidden by law.

209

Look at the diagram below, and then answer the question that follows.

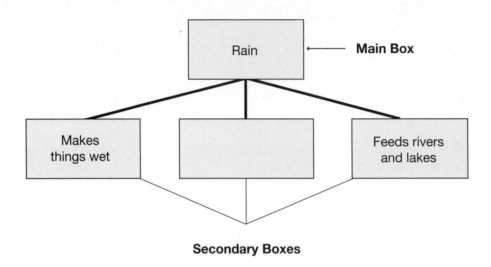

Using what you read in the previous passage, write which information should appear in the empty box in the diagram.

_____

_____

_____

 In a graphic organizer like this, supporting details appear in branched-out boxes.

Charts like the one in the last example are good ways to identify the main topic of a passage and the passage's supporting details. Why? Because they show a type of hierarchy. The main idea or topic appears in the top box, and all the supporting details appear in individual boxes that branch out underneath or to the sides.

Example 1

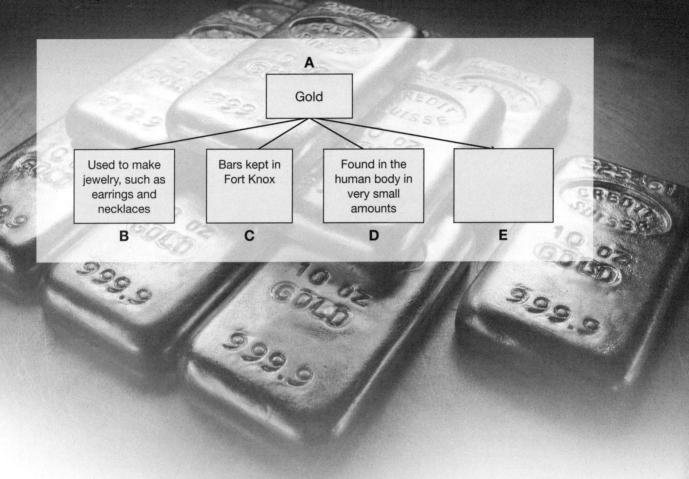

In the chart above, which of the following boxes holds the main idea?

A A

B C

C D

D E

Remember that the main topic should appear in the top or main box in a graphic organizer.

1b **In the chart above, a supporting detail for Box E could be**

F industry

G silver

H traded like money

J bronze

One of these choices is specific to the main topic.

Example 2

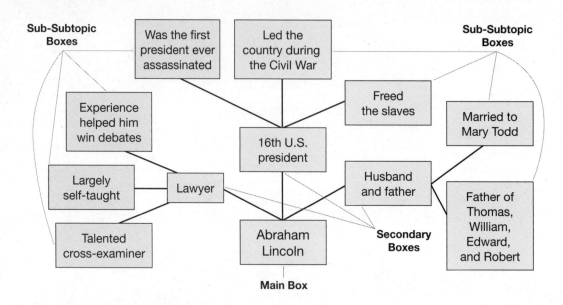

Sub-Subtopic Boxes

Was the first president ever assassinated

Led the country during the Civil War

Sub-Subtopic Boxes

Freed the slaves

Experience helped him win debates

Married to Mary Todd

16th U.S. president

Largely self-taught

Lawyer

Husband and father

Father of Thomas, William, Edward, and Robert

Talented cross-examiner

Abraham Lincoln

Secondary Boxes

Main Box

---

2 Write a paragraph using the graphic organizer above. Remember to first identify the main topic, then choose supporting details. Use your own paper if you need extra space.

_____

_____

_____

_____

_____

_____

_____

SELF Coach

Discuss your answer with your teacher or class.

Standard: S1.I.2.C Organize information according to an identifiable structure, such as compare/contrast or general to specific.

Coached Reading

The following passage is about two ancient civilizations. As you read the passage, use the statements and questions in the margin to help your understanding.

READ ALOUD Your teacher may read this selection to you.

Ancient Greece and Ancient Rome

by Carla Bambini

Life as we know it didn't happen overnight. It started many, many years ago, with two ancient civilizations. These are ancient Greece and ancient Rome. On separate paths, each had an approach to government, housing, and worship that has affected the way people live today. Sometimes, those approaches were alike. Sometimes, they differed greatly.

Ancient Greece, which existed over 2,000 years ago, was important to history. The people of that ancient civilization are responsible for developing what we know today as democracy. This way of life allowed people to take part in their government, or even shape it.

Overall, the ancient Greeks lived simply. There were two main cities—Sparta and Athens—where the Greeks built their homes. These homes, made of brick and stone, were built around open courtyards. This style of building can still be seen today. The ancient Greeks ate only twice a day. The Greeks called the morning or breakfast meal "ariston." It usually included things like beans or peas. In the evenings, they ate what they called "deipnon." This was a large but simple meal of cheese, olives, bread, and meat.

> What kind of structure has this paragraph adopted?

> What is the main idea of this paragraph?

> In this paragraph, what are some supporting details? Circle a few.

The Greeks dressed simply, too. Often, their only clothes were cloaks and sandals. Most parts of their life were simple, but they worshipped many goddesses and gods. To honor their gods, the Greeks built temples. One of the most famous was the Parthenon, also called the Temple of Athena. The Greeks honored their gods in other ways, as well. Back then, they were festivals to honor the gods. But today we know them universally as the Olympics.

Like Greece, ancient Rome existed thousands of years ago. We can still find remnants of that ancient civilization today. Both civilizations felt equal government was important. The ancient Greeks founded democracy, but the ancient Romans established a law principle used today. They called it "equity." That means a law should be flexible enough to fit different situations.

The houses the Romans lived in were, like the Greek homes, pretty simple. The center was a large, four-sided room called an "atrium." Other rooms were built around it. The center rooms were much like the Greeks' center courtyards. For meals, though, the Romans differed. They, unlike the Greeks, ate three meals a day.

The ancient Roman's usual attire consisted of comfortable tunics we call "togas" today. Like the Greeks, the Romans worshipped many goddesses and gods. The Romans took many Greek goddesses and gods and gave them new names. The Greek goddess Aphrodite, for example, became the Roman goddess Venus.

The Romans, like the Greeks, liked to celebrate with festivals. Usually, these affairs were held in a huge open theater called the Colosseum. Like the Greeks' Parthenon, the Colosseum is still standing. One of the most popular events there was the chariot races. They were held in a large arena called a "circus." The largest circus in ancient Rome was the Circus Maximus. It entertained roughly 180,000 Romans.

The ancient Greeks had the Olympics, the ancient Romans, the circus. Both civilizations built homes, made meals, chose clothes, held festivals. In many ways they were different, but they were both models for our life today.

Which things here are general? Which are specific?

How do the ancient civilizations compare and contrast? As you read, circle some examples.

What is the main topic of this paragraph? How does it use compare and contrast?

Reread the passage, and ask yourself the questions in the margin again. Then do Numbers 1 through 6.

1 What is a piece of general information in the third paragraph?

A   "Ariston" was the morning meal.

B   The ancient Greeks ate twice a day.

C   At night, the ancient Greeks ate meat.

D   The ancient Greeks lived simply.

2 The main idea of the second paragraph is that

F   Ancient Greece had a form of government.

G   Democracy is a form of government.

H   Ancient Greece was an important civilization.

J   Governments existed 2,000 years ago.

3 How did the houses of each group compare? Write your answer on the lines below.

_____

_____

_____

4 The Ancient Greeks and Ancient Romans had the same approach to

A clothing

B god worship

C meals

D chariot races

5 Which of the following is the most specific piece of information in the passage overall?

F Ancient Greece was an ancient civilization.

G Life started many years ago.

H There were ancient civilizations.

J Ancient Greece founded the Olympics.

6 What is the main idea of the passage? Use two specific examples to support your response. Write your answer on the lines below.

_____

_____

_____

Discuss your answer with your teacher or class

Test Practice

Read the following passage about alligators and crocodiles. Then do Numbers 1 through 3.

The animal kingdom is a vast place. It's got frogs and toads, bison and buffalo, crickets and grasshoppers. These animals are often confused with each other! Perhaps the animals most commonly confused are alligators and crocodiles. With a little practice, though, most people can tell them apart.

In some basic ways, alligators and crocodiles are alike. They're both types of crocodilians, and, at first glance, they look very similar. They have bumpy skin, short legs, and long tails, as well as cold blood and snaggle teeth. Both eat meat and can live on land and water.

Alligators and crocodiles have certain distinctions, though. The most notable one is the shape of their mouths. An alligator tends to have a wide and U-shaped mouth. A crocodile's mouth, however, is pointy and V-shaped. The teeth of each are distinct as well. With alligators, only the upper teeth are visible when the mouth is shut. With crocodiles, in contrast, you can clearly see both sets of teeth.

Some of the physical differences between the two are harder to spot. For example, crocodiles have salt glands on their tongues that allow them to get rid of excess salt. Alligators do not. Crocodiles also have sense organs that look like little black dots on every scale on their bodies. Alligators have organs like this, too, but only on their heads and jaws.

1 What is the main idea of the passage?

A Every crocodile has salt glands.

B Pointy teeth are a sign of a crocodile.

C Alligators and crocodiles eat meat.

D Alligators and crocodiles can be told apart.

2 Alligators and crocodiles are similar in that they have

F bumpy skin

G sense organs all over their bodies.

H the same teeth

J salt glands

3 What is the general idea of the second paragraph? Give two or three examples to prove your point.

_____

_____

_____

Read the following letters from two pen pals. Then do Numbers 4 through 6.

1.

Dear Lucy:

My name is Lee, and I'm almost 11 years old. My parents and I live in Beijing, China, in a high-rise apartment building. It's a busy city with lots to do—but crowded sidewalks!

Unlike some of my friends, I like school. Art and Chinese are my favorite, but I don't like math. For fun, I like drawing, eating, and watching TV. Sometimes, I also like reading.

I want to be a fashion designer when I grow up. I want to make beautiful clothes for people to wear. What about you?

I'm so glad I have a pen pal from another country. Please write soon!

Lee

2.

Dear Lee:

I'm so excited to have a pen pal in China—thank you for writing! Your city sounds very exciting. Your life does, too! Overall, my life is pretty boring.

I live in a one-floor house in Ghana, and it's quiet. But I live with my parents, like you. And I almost forgot: my grandmother lives with us, too!

I don't have many hobbies—I told you I was boring. I even have to wear a uniform to school.

So that's about it. Please write again soon—Your letters are the most exciting part of my day!

Lucy

4 What is one specific idea of Lucy's letter?

  A that her life is boring

  B that she has to wear a uniform to school

  C that she's excited to have a pen pal

  D that she's thankful to Lee for writing

5 Lee lives in a

  F crowded sidewalk

  G high-rise apartment building

  H one-floor house

  J fashion warehouse

6 How do the lives of Lee and Lucy compare? What details could you add to each to make them more or less similar? Use specific examples.

_____

_____

_____

_____

_____

_____

_____

_____

_____

_____

_____

_____

_____

_____

Standards: S1.I.2.A Produce oral and written reports on topics related to all school subjects.

S1.I.2.E Use the process of prewriting, drafting, revising, and proofreading (the "writing process") to produce well-constructed informational texts.

CHAPTER 7

The Stages of Writing

Lesson 28: The Writing Process: Prewriting

It's pretty easy to write a correct sentence. It takes a little more thought, and time, to write a paragraph, but you can manage it. What about writing a two-page essay? Does that seem like a big leap? Don't worry—it's not. In this chapter, you'll learn how to start an essay, as well as ways to get through writing that essay step by step. The first step is to find a topic.

Let's say you're asked to write about your favorite season. First, jot down ideas about each season. What do you like? Not like? You could make a list for each season and pick the season with the longest list. Or maybe there's no question about which is the best. You just have to try to express why you like it.

A useful tool for pinning down your thoughts about a topic is the graphic organizer. A **graphic organizer** is a picture that helps you organize your ideas.

THINKING IT THROUGH Read the passage below, and then answer the question that follows.

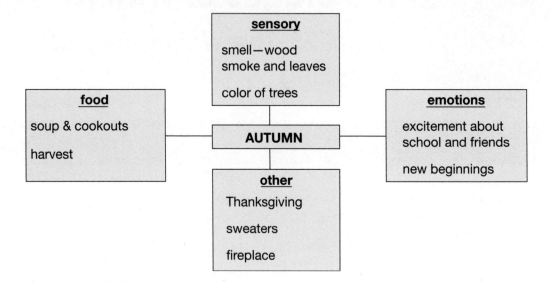

What will be the subject of this piece of writing?

_____

_____

_____

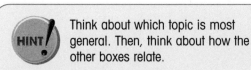 **HINT!** Think about which topic is most general. Then, think about how the other boxes relate.

The middle box of a graphic organizer holds the main topic—in this case, autumn. The boxes around the middle box all hold ideas about that topic—by categories.

To start your own graphic organizer, first draw a box or circle in the center of a page. Then, write your main topic in that box. Next, draw lines from that box to new, empty boxes. You'll use these surrounding boxes to brainstorm ideas for your essay.

As you start thinking about how to write your essay, you'll start to see some patterns in your ideas. Group your ideas into categories, then use the graphic organizer to visualize your essay. In other words, try to put similar ideas in the same box. This will help you start to determine how many paragraphs your essay will have.

Standards: S1.I.2.A Produce oral and written reports on topics related to all school subjects.

S1.I.2.E Use the process of prewriting, drafting, revising, and proofreading (the "writing process") to produce well-constructed informational texts.

Lesson 29
The Writing Process: Drafting

Writing an essay can seem tough, but if you break the process into bite-sized pieces, it all comes together pretty easily. One way to do this is by drafting one paragraph at a time.

To start, use the idea web you created in the last lesson to determine how many paragraphs you'll have and what they'll be about. You should have introductory and concluding paragraphs, and supporting paragraphs in between.

Writing Introductions

Use the **introductory paragraph** to interest your readers and explain your essay topic. Here's one possible introduction:

> "There was only one truly great actress: Katharine Hepburn."

Near or at the end of your introductory paragraph, write a **thesis statement** that explains your essay's main point and its structure. Consider the sample below:

> "Katharine Hepburn is my hero because of her acting achievements, independent spirit, and deep intelligence."

From this example, you can guess the three supporting paragraphs and their order.

Writing Supporting Paragraphs

After you write a good thesis statement, it's time to start writing the paragraphs that support your statement. For each paragraph, first state the topic, then include specific examples. As you move between paragraphs, be sure to use transitions. They help your reader follow your thoughts.

Writing Conclusions

Now you're almost done. You've stated a point and supported that point with specific examples in logical order. Now write a conclusion to wrap everything up. Restate your major points and put your argument in perspective.

Because it restates the essay's major points, the conclusion is like the thesis statement, so that part's pretty easy. When you restate those points, though, try to use slightly different words. "Restate" does not mean "repeat."

The second part of writing a conclusion involves putting it all in perspective. This part is a bit harder but more fun. Ask yourself, "Why does this point matter?"

So that's all there is to drafting an essay: an introduction with a thesis statement, supporting paragraphs with lots of specific examples, and a conclusion that puts it all in perspective.

 THINKING IT THROUGH Read the passage below, and then answer the question that follows.

Some people get excited in the spring, because they're eager to clean their houses and plant their gardens. Some dislike school. Their most content during summer vacation. Everybody has a favorite season. Autumn is my favorite season for how it smells, looks, and feels and for how it tastes.

People sense it as soon as he or she step outside in October: autumn looks, smells, and feels terrific! Trees that are normally green suddenly turn colors. The air smells good. Maple syrup is my favorite food! During the day, the temperature is warm but not too warm. At night, you can wear your favorite sweaters as the air starts to get a little chilly.

As good as autumn looks, smells, and feels, it tastes even better. In autumn, you get the best of summer foods. You can still cook out and get vegetables like corn on the cob. You can get the first foods of winter, too. Things like hot, spicy cider and hearty, tangy chili. Best of all, though, are the tastes of Thanksgiving. What better way to celebrate autumn than with turkey, stuffing, and all the fixings?

In autumn, we start school. With new supplies, we meet new friends and see old ones we missed during the summer. Also, as the days grow colder and shorter, we have more time to enjoy new movie and television shows after a summer of reruns.

New Yorkers like me know best: autumn is a wonderful season. It's definitely the season for food. It offers summer foods like corn on the cob and winter foods like chili. The best thing about autumn, though, is what it means: a new school year, reuniting with friends, and new movies and television shows.

How would you change the introduction of this essay to make it better?

_____

_____

_____

Now you're ready to try drafting. On your own paper, draft your own essay. Be sure to include:

- **a clear thesis statement**
- **at least two paragraphs with detailed examples**
- **transitions between paragraphs**
- **an introduction and a conclusion**

Standards: S1.I.2.A   Produce oral and written reports on topics related to all school subjects.
S1.I.2.E   Use the process of prewriting, drafting, revising, and proofreading (the "writing process") to produce well-constructed informational texts.

Lesson 30
The Writing Process: Revising

Have you ever read an essay a teacher handed back to you and thought, "Why did I write that?" or, "How could I make a mistake like that?" You can avoid those feelings by reviewing and revising your work. **Reviewing** means reading your work, while **revising** means changing it. These steps are part of the editing process, and editing is a very important part of writing. It can mean the difference between a so-so paper and a great one.

You start revising after you write a first draft of your essay. At this point, you've got an introduction, a thesis statement, supporting paragraphs, and a conclusion. You should be proud and relieved. The tough part's done.

Before you start revising, though, take the time to reread your essay. As you reread, ask yourself these basic editing questions:

- **Do I have a clear thesis statement?** Check for a thesis statement toward the end of your introductory paragraph. Make sure it states your main point clearly and forecasts the structure of your paper.

- **Have I included everything I need to support my point?** You should have a paragraph on each of your supporting points with clear, specific examples.

- **Do I have an introduction and a conclusion?** Does your introductory paragraph grab readers' attention and interest them the topic? Does it clearly lay out the points to follow? Does your concluding paragraph restate your main points and put the whole essay in perspective?

- **Is my structure clear and helpful?** Have you chosen the best way to organize your points? Would another way be clearer or more interesting? Does one paragraph or sentence seem not to fit?

When revising, always check that you've ordered your paragraphs logically. If you move any, reread them all to make sure they still make sense. Often, you'll have to change transitions, too, because you're linking different paragraphs.

Once you've done that, look closely at the sentences in each paragraph. Consider the topics and examples you've used. Make sure you need all the sentences and don't need any others and make sure those sentences are also ordered correctly. Sometimes, reordering sentences can make a paragraph much clearer. Put the sentence that tells what the paragraph is about at the beginning, for example.

Read the passage below, which is the later version of the passage on page 224. Then answer the question that follows.

Some people get excited in the spring, because they're eager to clean their houses and plant their gardens. Some dislike school. Their happiest during summer vacation. Everybody has a favorite season. Autumn is my favorite season for how it smells, looks, and feels; for how it tastes; and, most important, for what it means.

People sense it as soon as he or she step outside in October: Autumn looks, smells, and feels terrific. Trees that are normally muted greens suddenly blaze in yellows, reds, and oranges. The air smells deliciously of rich wood smoke and damp Maple leaves. During the day, the temperature is warm enough to go without a coat yet cool enough not to worry about sweating. At night, you can wear your favorite sweaters as the air starts to get a little chilly.

As good as autumn looks, smells, and feels, it tastes even better. In autumn, you get the best of summer foods. You can still cook out and get vegetables like corn on the cob. You can get the first foods of winter, too. Things like hot, spicy cider and hearty, tangy chili. Best of all, though, are the tastes of Thanksgiving. What better way to celebrate autumn than with turkey, stuffing, and all the fixings?

Thanksgiving is just one of the events that makes autumn special. In autumn, we start school. With new supplies, we meet new friends and see old ones we missed during the summer. Also, as the days grow colder and shorter, we have more time to enjoy new movie and television shows after a summer of reruns.

New yorkers like me know best: Autumn is a wonderful season. It's sights, smells, and feel can be dazzling, refreshing, and even comforting. It's definitely the season for food, too. It offers summer foods like corn on the cob and winter foods like chili. The best thing about autumn, though, is what it means: a new school year, reuniting with friends, and new movies and television shows. If you're ever tired of the ice and snow and plan to move to an eternal-summer spot like California, ask yourself, "Would I miss autumn?" I know I would.

NOTICE: Photocopying any part of this book is forbidden by law.

227

What are some ways in which the author revised this essay? Were they good changes? Explain why.

_____

_____

_____

_____

_____

Now return to the essay you wrote in the last lesson and revise it, as well.

Standards: S1.I.2.A Produce oral and written reports on topics related to all school subjects.

S1.I.2.E Use the process of prewriting, drafting, revising, and proofreading (the "writing process") to produce well-constructed informational texts.

Lesson 31
The Writing Process: Proofreading and Editing

Once you revise your essay and make any big changes, reorganize paragraphs or add specifics, for example, take another break if you can. You must be fresh when you sit down for the next step: proofreading. During **proofreading**, you look for errors in spelling, capitalization, punctuation, verb agreement, and formatting. These kinds of errors are easy to correct.

But won't your readers understand you whether you spell *whether* right or not? Probably, but why risk it? If you use *where* where you meant to use *wear*, you might confuse your readers. At the least, you'll distract them, because they'll pause to correct your error in their heads. If your readers aren't forgiving, they might think less of you for your haste and sloppiness, and not care about what you wrote because they think you did less than your best.

Here's a checklist that should help you proofread and edit your work.

Editing Checklist

1   Check your capitalization and punctuation.

2   Spell all words correctly.

3   Check for sentence fragments and run-on sentences.

4   Keep verb tense consistent.

5   Make sure subjects and verbs agree.

6   Use words according to the rules of standard English.

7   Remember to break paragraphs correctly.

Read the passage below, which is a later version of a passage you read in the last lesson. Then answer the question that follows.

Some people get excited in the spring, because they're eager to clean their houses and plant their gardens. Some dislike school. They're most content during summer vacation. Everybody has a favorite season. Autumn is my favorite season for how it smells, looks, and feels; for how it tastes; and, most important, for what it means.

People sense it as soon as they step outside in October: Autumn looks, smells, and feels terrific. Trees that are normally muted greens suddenly blaze in yellows, reds, and oranges. The air smells deliciously of rich wood smoke and damp maple leaves. During the day, the temperature is warm enough to go out without a coat yet cool enough not to worry about sweating. At night, you can wear your favorite sweaters as the air starts to get a little chilly.

As good as autumn looks, smells, and feels, it tastes even better. In autumn, you get the best of summer foods. You can still cook out and get vegetables like corn on the cob. You can get the first foods of winter, too, things like hot, spicy cider and hearty, tangy chili. Best of all, though, are the tastes of Thanksgiving. What better way to celebrate autumn than with turkey, stuffing, and all the fixings?

Thanksgiving is just one of the events that makes autumn special. In autumn, we start school. With new supplies, we meet new friends and see old ones we missed during the summer. Also, as the days grow colder and shorter, we have more time to enjoy new movies and television shows after a summer of reruns.

New Yorkers like me know best: Autumn is a wonderful season. Its sights, smells, and feel can be dazzling, refreshing, and even comforting. It's definitely the season for food, too. It offers summer foods like corn on the cob and winter foods like chili. The best thing about autumn, though, is what it means: a new school year, reuniting with friends, and new movies and television shows. If you're ever tired of the ice and snow and plan to move to an eternal-summer spot like California, ask yourself, "Would I miss autumn?" I know I would.

If you were proofreading this essay, what are some things you would fix? Use at least two or three specific examples.

_____

_____

_____

Now return to the essay you revised in the last lesson and proofread that, too.

 230

Lesson 32
The Writing Process: Preparing a Bibliography

When you're writing, it's very important to record the sources you used for information. You should always make sure the right people are getting credit for that information, and that your readers will be able to find your sources.

When you're researching a topic, be sure to take down all the bibliographic information you need before returning your reference materials to the library or visiting another website. **Bibliographic information** is the information you put in a bibliography, which is an alphabetical list of sources at the end of your essay or paper. Your bibliography may include books, encyclopedia entries, magazine articles, Internet sources, and more.

Below are examples of how to list different sources in a bibliography. Different teachers and even reference books show these sources in slightly different ways. And that's okay. Just remember these two important things:

1. When in doubt, include as much information as you can so your readers will be certain where to find your source; and
2. Be consistent. Make sure, for instance, that all the book listings match.

Books

Note that the author's last name is always listed first. With two authors, the second name is listed first name first. After that comes the title, city of publication, publisher's name, and year of publication. Look on the title page for this information.

McLaughlin, Michael. *The Manhattan Chili Co. Southwest-American Cookbook: A Spicy Pot of Chilies, Fixins', and Other Regional Favorites*. New York: Crown Publishers, 1986.

Hayward, Linda, and James Watling. *The First Thanksgiving*. New York: Random House, 1990.

Note that titles of long works, like books, encyclopedias, and magazines, are either underlined when written by hand or italicized when typed on the computer. The titles of articles or entries are placed in quotation marks.

NOTICE: Photocopying any part of this book is forbidden by law.

231

Encyclopedias

Usually, there is no author for an encyclopedia entry. Therefore, the entry title listed first.

"Maple." *Encyclopedia Americana*, vol.18, 2001.

"Cider." *Encyclopedia Britannica*, vol. 3, 2002.

Internet Sources

Make sure with Internet sources that you list the date you found the information. The final piece of an Internet bibliographic entry should be the Web address, so your reader can find it.

"The Chemistry of Autumn Colors." Chemical of the Week. Online. Internet 15 January 2005. Available at http://scifun.chem.wisc.edu/chemweek/fallcolr/fallcolr.html

"The First Thanksgiving." Scholastic Web site. Online. Internet 16 January 2005. Available http://teacher.scholastic.com/thanksgiving/

Interviews

When including an interview in your bibliography, you can put "interview with author," "telephone conversation with author," or "e-mail exchange with author" to be specific. Make sure to include the date of the interview.

Costanza, Muriel. Telephone interview with author, 28 January 2005.

Newspaper and Magazine Articles

With newspaper and magazine articles, put the author first, then the title of the article in quotation marks. The final information in the bibliographic entry for an article is the page numbers. That makes it easy for a reader to find.

Cunningham, Bill. "Autumn Mix." *The New York Times* 31 October 2004: ST4(L).

Ford, Oma Blaise. "November: Celebrate the Season by Gathering Family and Friends around a Delectably Decorated Harvest Table." *Better Homes and Gardens* November 2004: 27.

Test Practice

The passage below needs editing. After reading it, use the accompanying editing checklist, then do Numbers 1 through 4.

Editing Checklist

1 Check your capitalization and punctuation.

2 Spell all words correctly.

3 Check for sentence fragments and run-on sentences.

4 Keep verb tense consistent.

5 Make sure subjects and verbs agree.

6 Use words according to the rules of standard English.

7 Remember to break paragraphs correctly.

Human babies have to be taken care of by someone they would die otherwise. Sometimes they have just one parent, but usually they have two. Turtles hatch from eggs in the ground and instinctively scratch their way up. Their born knowing how to feed and protect themselves. Baby wolfs, on the other hand, is taken care of by two parents. The Mother and Father take turns hunting for food and guarding their children. Unlike human babies some animal babies grow up without a parent's help.

1 Which word is incorrect in the following sentence from the passage?

> **Turtles hatch from eggs in the ground and instinctively scratches their way up.**

A scratches

B turtles

C their

D hatch

2 Which sentence has incorrect subject/verb agreement?

F Sometimes they have just one parent, but usually they have two.

G Unlike human babies some animal babies grow up without a parent's help.

H The mother and father take turns hunting for food and guarding their children.

J Baby wolfs, on the other hand, is taken care of by two parents.

3 What is wrong with the following sentence from the passage?

> **Human babies have to be taken care of by someone they would die otherwise.**

A It's a fragment.

B The subject and verb don't agree.

C It's a run-on sentence.

D The subject is spelled incorrectly.

4 List three errors in the passage, and explain how to fix them.

_____

_____

_____

The passage below is an essay that needs editing. Read it and, using the editing checklist, do Numbers 5 through 8.

I still learn something about cooking every time I go to the soup kitchen. I learned to mix really well, with all kinds of bowls and spoons. How important clean bowls are. Now I always get my parents to polish theres. I learned about salad. Its always difficult to cook lots of rice. My sister is a terrible cook. Sometimes I learn what not to do. I've even learned to make my own recipes. They're simple, but good. I've learned a lot about making food at the soup kitchen.

5 The sentence that should start the passage is

F "I've learned a lot about making food at the soup kitchen."

G "I've even learned to make my own recipes."

H "I learned about salad."

J "I learned to mix really well, with all kinds of bowls and spoons."

6 What is wrong with the following sentence?

Its always difficult to cook lots of rice.

A subject/verb agreement

B spelling

C punctuation

D capitalization

7 Which sentence does <u>not</u> belong in the passage?

F "How important clean bowls are."

G "My sister is a terrible cook."

H "I learned about salad."

J "Sometimes I learn what not to do."

8 Write one or two sentences that add specific examples to the passage. If needed, edit sentences already in the passage.

_____

_____

_____

_____

_____

_____

Standard: S3.I.2.A Present (in essays, position papers, speeches, and debates) clear analyses of issues, ideas, texts, and experiences, supporting their positions with well-developed arguments.

CHAPTER

Writing Other Nonfiction

Lesson 33: Writing an Editorial or Letter to the Editor

Sometimes, you'll feel really strongly about an issue—strongly enough to write something called an **editorial** or a **letter to the editor**. You use these types of writing to express your opinions or reactions to news or events. You learned about opinions in Chapter 5, so you understand that these types of writing aren't purely informational, like textbooks. They're types of writing that are usually also meant to persuade.

While editorials usually take sides on an issue, they don't have to. But what they all are designed to do is:

- Explain a complicated issue
- Let readers know about an important issue or activity
- Express an opinion
- Catch readers' interest and get them thinking about an issue

Look at the following example of an editorial:

> King James of England is unfairly forcing his subjects to join the Church of England. And if they refuse, he either puts them in jail or throws them out of the country. His decision makes no sense. England can't be stable with so much unrest. King James must rethink his position.

What's the author's main message? That King James is treating his subjects unfairly. You can immediately tell the author disagrees with King James. King James is described as "unfair" in the very first sentence. The author also provides reasons for the opinion: the treatment is too strict and it threatens the country's stability. A good editorial doesn't just state an opinion. It backs up the opinion with reasons behind that point of view, and it tells readers the desired course of action.

So let's try to write an editorial. What's our first step?

Choose an Issue

The first thing we need to do is choose an issue. An editorial should be something you feel strongly about, whether it's the environment, school sports, an endangered species, or something that just happened. Whatever topic you choose, make sure you have an opinion about it, one you feel you can support. Consider the following topic and opinion:

> **Role models**
> Kids should pick positive ones.

This author has decided to write about why kids should have positive role models.

What topic will you write your editorial about? What's your opinion? Write your answer on the lines below.

_____

_____

_____

Explain the Other Side of the Issue

As you learned in Chapter 5, a strong argument is one that addresses the other side's argument. The same holds true for an editorial. At the very least, you should mention the other side's point of view. That way, your readers will know you're aware of it—and they'll be aware of it, too. Look at the following example:

> Some people feel that role models aren't important.

As you can see, this author acknowledges that some people have a different view.

What's the other side of your opinion or view? Write your answer on the lines below.

_____

_____

_____

Gather Support

Once you have your topic and have acknowledged the other side's view, what's next? Gathering information to support your position. At this stage, gather as many facts as you can. Also, try to think of ways to connect with your audience. Remember, as you learned in Chapter 5, a fact is something you can prove, and an argument that connects with the reader is a stronger one.

Look at the example below:

> Not all kids choose good role models.
>
> Some kids are choosing role models who are cartoon characters or actors who don't always do good things.
>
> Poor role models can hurt kids, while good ones can help them.

These are some of the reasons this author has chosen to use when writing the editorial. But there are more. Don't limit yourself.

How would you support your opinion or view? Write your answer on the lines below.

_____

_____

_____

Now you're ready to put your editorial together. On your own paper, draft your editorial. Be sure to include:

- a clear thesis statement
- at least two paragraphs with detailed examples
- transitions between paragraphs
- an introduction and a conclusion

Lesson 34
Writing a News Story

When you want to learn about the day's events, where do you turn? Many of us turn to the newspaper. Why? Because **newspapers** provide facts about current events—and they're written for wide audiences, so they're generally easy to read.

Writing a news story isn't like other types of writing, though. It's got two very distinct parts:

- Lead—the first sentence that summarizes the story
- Body—all the facts that support the story

The lead sentence is a very important part of a news story, because it starts the story and tells readers all the story's critical information. Specifically, the lead includes something called the "5 Ws and 1 H," which stands for:

- Who
- What
- Where
- When
- Why
- How

The body of the story then goes on to give details about all those things. Look at the following example of a lead:

> At about 5 PM yesterday at her 77 Oak View Lane home, police arrested Sylvia Smith for operating an illegal candy store on the premises for the past 11 years. Smith did not struggle, so the police were able to arrest her peacefully.

From this example, one of the first "W"s, "when," is clear. Sylvia was arrested at 5 PM yesterday. And that's two more "W"s: "who" and "what." "Who" is Sylvia Smith and "what" is "arrested." Where was she arrested? We know this, too—at her home at 77 Oak View Lane. So what does that leave? Why—which is the last "W." That's because she was operating an illegal candy store. And the "H" of the lead—"how" did it happen? Peacefully, because Sylvia didn't struggle.

So you can see that writing a news lead can be rather simple—as long as you remember to include all the pieces. There are many pieces—so many, in fact, that sometimes the author breaks them into more than one sentence. This is okay—something you can do, too—just try not to use too many.

 Read the passage below, and then answer the question that follows.

Yesterday, a package fell from the sky, hitting a man at 4 Yellowstone Lane on the head.

Which part or parts of the lead are missing here? How would you rewrite this lead to make it better?

_____

_____

_____

 HINT Are all the "5 Ws and 1H" represented? What parts do you need to fill in?

Example 1

MAN ACCUSED OF DOG THEFT

By Martha Master, senior staff writer

HARLEIGH, Calif.—Stan Kemp, of 43 Poacher Lane, was arrested yesterday on charges of dog-napping. Kemp is accused of running a ring of dog-nappers who steal and resell show dogs.

He was arrested yesterday afternoon, after Peanut, a champion beagle, was spotted in his yard. Peanut belongs to John Brubeck, who alerted the police once he located his dog.

John Brubeck reunited with his dog, Peanut

1a **In this passage, what is the event that occurred?**

A John Brubeck found his dog.

B Peanuts was returned to his owner.

C Stan Kemp was arrested for dog-napping.

D Stan Kemp ran a ring of dog-nappers.

Think carefully about what this story is about. Why is the author writing this story?

1b **What is the "H" (the "how") of this passage?**

F John found Peanuts and alerted police.

G Peanuts found his way home and John called police.

H The police found Peanuts and went to Stan.

J Stan turned himself in to police.

Reread the passage carefully to determine how the events occurred.

Example 2

LOCAL RESIDENT WINS BALLOONING AWARD

By Jeff Paster, staff writer

BALLSTON SPA, NY—Local resident Sandy Hill, of 44 Peach Tree Lane, was awarded the nation's highest ballooning award. Hill said she was honored to accept the award before the night's 200-person crowd, because it was her first in a 17-year career. She got the award last night at the Ballston Spa Hilton.

2 **Rewrite this story with a better lead.**

_____

_____

_____

_____

_____

_____

_____

_____

_____

_____

_____

Lesson 35
Writing a Review

Some people get paid to write about the things they've seen or read—and why they did or did not like those things. A **review** is a piece of writing that describes the work and tells how the reader or viewer felt about it. So these are the two parts of a good review:

- summary of the book or film
- reviewer's opinion of the book or film

Consider the following review of a famous book:

> A long journey. A new home. Fighting to protect yourself. Sound interesting? It is. It's *Watership Down* by Richard Adams.
>
> In this book, a group of adventurous rabbits have to flee their home when a local land developer threatens to destroy it. One of the group's young rabbits, Fiver, tries to warn the chief rabbit—but to no avail. No one believes Fiver, actually. No one, that is, except his big brother, Hazel.
>
> So a small band of rabbits—with Fiver at the helm—set out on a long journey to find a safe home, by themselves. They eventually find it, only to realize there are no females in their group. How can they survive now? They then plot to help another group of rabbits escape their harsh and cruel chief. Do they succeed? Read on and find out.
>
> With vivid details, danger, and excitement, *Watership Down* is a book you won't put down. Adams has written a story that is entertaining and believable. This uplifting and exciting tale is a story about loyalty and courage that will stay with readers long after the last page.

As you can see, the author of this review starts by catching the reader's interest. That's a good way to get readers to read on. But then the author tells what happens in the book. This should happen early in a review. It's not necessary to tell all the events of the book. You just tell enough of the plot to interest readers.

So don't give everything away, but certainly tell the main events—things like the conflict and the climax. After that, as the author did here, tell the readers why you did or did not like the book. Remember, a review is designed to share an opinion. When you're writing a review, don't just share your opinion—share *why* you have it.

 Read the passage below, and then answer the question that follows.

Last week, I saw the movie *My Horse's Life*. In it, the main character, Carol, tells about the life of her horse, Jamille. She starts at the beginning, telling how and when she got Jamille. Then, she tells about all the adventures the two had together. Carol and her horse attended many horse shows, for example, and together they gave many, many riding lessons to young children.

What is missing from this review? What would you add to make it better? Write your answer on the lines below.

_____

_____

_____

 A well-written review contains two parts: a summary of events of the book or film and the reviewer's opinion of those events.

Now you're ready to try writing a review yourself. Pick a book you've read or a movie you've seen recently. Then write a review of it. As you do, remember to include:

- summary of the book or movie's main events
- your opinion of the book or movie
- why you have your opinion

Write your review on the lines below.

_____

_____

_____

_____

_____

_____

_____

_____

_____

_____

_____

_____

_____

_____

_____

_____

Lesson 36
Answering
Constructed-Response Questions

On the New York State English Language Arts test, you'll be asked to answer short-answer questions. These questions require two or three lines of answers. But don't be alarmed. This is easier to do than you might think.

Before you start answering these types of questions, though, it's important that you understand how you'll be graded on them. This table shows how these answers are scored.

Score	To get this score, you—
5	• discussed the correct element of the passage • interpreted the passage thoroughly • made connections beyond the text, if possible • developed your ideas fully • used relevant and accurate examples from the passage
4	• discussed the important elements of the passage • analyzed the passage • made connections beyond the text, if possible • gave an answer long enough to answer the question • gave some examples and details from the passage • may have included some mistakes
3	• answered the question partially • discussed the important elements of the passage incompletely • showed gaps in understanding of the passage • made some connections • gave a short answer • did not give enough examples from the text • may have included some mistakes

Score table continued

2	• answered the question partially • showed that you noticed important points but did not discuss them • did not show understanding of the whole passage • did not make connections beyond the passage • gave few examples • may have included some mistakes
1	• did not do what the question asked you to do • dealt with little of the actual passage • did not show that you understood the passage • made no connections beyond the passage • gave almost no examples, or none • made mistakes in fact or grammar
0	• Gave an answer that made no sense at all.

As you can tell from this table, your score will depend on how completely you answer the question. The more information you include, the better you'll do and the higher your score will be.

Look at the following passage. Imagine you found this passage on your language arts test, followed by these questions.

Daniela lingered in front of the tomato vines, unsure what to do. She was so proud of these tomatoes. The rest of the garden was doing well, too. But these tomatoes really took the prize. They were getting plump, red, and shiny. She'd worked hard to ensure they'd grow large and full.

But her family was about to move, and the tomatoes still wouldn't be ready to pick. Who would take care of her precious tomatoes? Weed them? Pick them? Should she get somebody to care for them, or should she take them with her? How would the plants survive a trip if they weren't ready to pick now? She didn't want to leave the plants, but she also didn't want to hurt them.

It was bad enough that Daniela would have to leave her friends, her school, and everything she'd ever known. She couldn't leave her tomatoes, too.

What problem does Daniela face? Why is she unsure what to do?

How would you go about getting a top score on this question? What kinds of things would you include? For an example, look at the following:

Example of a Top—Scoring Response—5 Points
Example
The problem Daniela faces is what to do about her tomatoes. She is unsure what to do—get someone to take care of them or take them with her—because she wants the best for her tomatoes, but she has put a lot of time into caring for them and would like to be able to pick them herself. She'd also like to see how they'd do next year.

For the most part, answers to questions like these will vary, but this answer addresses both parts of the question, and addresses them well. It describes the problem Daniela faces, the choices she's struggling with, and why she's unsure which choice to make. This is the kind of answer that earns a top score. It's complete and includes all the needed information, nothing more.

Example 1

Each year for the past 100 years, the earth has grown warmer by one degree Fahrenheit. Many scientists believe this trend will continue, and they're growing concerned. If it does continue, they say, the Earth's climate will change, and then life as we know it will have to change.

Scientists call this phenomenon "global warming." When something burns, like fuel in a car, carbon dioxide enters the air. That carbon dioxide keeps the sun's heat from escaping the Earth, and then the earth gets warmer and warmer.

Many scientists believe the only way to stop global warming is to cut down on the amount of carbon dioxide in the air. To do this, though, people everywhere would have to find new ways to stop pollution.

---

1 **What causes global warming, and why does it have some scientists concerned?**

_____

_____

_____

_____

_____

_____

SELF Coach   Discuss your answer with your teacher or class.

Lesson 37
Answering Open-Ended Questions

In the last lesson, you learned the best ways to answer short-answer questions. In this lesson, we'll help you tackle questions of a different kind: open-ended questions, or questions that require more than three lines of answers. Remember the scoring table you saw in Lesson 36? These questions are scored slightly differently.

Here's another table:

Score	To get this score, you—
5	<ul><li>discussed the correct element of the passage</li><li>interpreted the passage thoroughly</li><li>made connections beyond the text, if possible</li><li>developed your ideas fully</li><li>used relevant and accurate examples from the passage</li><li>established and kept a clear focus</li><li>showed a logical sequence of ideas</li><li>wrote an answer that was easy to read</li><li>used different kinds of sentences and good vocabulary</li></ul>
4	<ul><li>discussed the important elements of the passage</li><li>analyzed the passage literally</li><li>made connections beyond the text, if possible</li><li>gave an answer long enough to answer the question</li><li>gave some examples and details from the passage</li><li>gave a focused answer, with some irrelevant details</li><li>showed an attempt at organization</li><li>wrote a readable response</li><li>used simple sentences and basic vocabulary</li><li>may have included some mistakes</li></ul>

Score	To get this score, you—
3	• answered the question partially • discussed the important elements of the passage incompletely • showed gaps in understanding of the passage • made some connections • gave a short answer • did not give enough examples from the text • may have included some mistakes • gave a fairly focused answer, but may have wandered off the topic • attempted to organize your answer • wrote a readable reponse • used simple sentences and basic vocabulary
2	• answered the question partially • showed that you noticed important points but did not discuss them • did not show understanding of the whole passage • did not make connections beyond the passage • gave few examples • may have included some mistakes • showed an attempt to focus the answer • may have included some unimportant information • did not organize the answer very effectively • wrote a readable but very dull answer • used little vocabulary • did not compose thoughts sufficiently
1	• did not do what the question asked you to do • dealt with little of the actual passage • did not show that you understood the passage • made no connections beyond the passage • gave almost no examples, or none • made mistakes with facts or grammar • did not try to establish a focus • focused on minor details or unimportant information • showed little attempt at organization • gave an answer that was difficult to read • used little vocabulary • did not focus your thoughts
0	• gave an answer that was illegible or completely off topic

Again, New York State grades you on how completely you answer open-ended questions, and in these types of questions, organization. Just as with short-answer questions, though, the more you include—the right information in the proper order—the better you'll do and the better your score. If you leave things out, your score will go down.

Think about the scoring table as you consider the following example:

> They started walking in February 1999. For twenty days, members of the Lakota Sioux and other Native American tribes walked and rode horses for 507 miles. They started from the Black Hills of South Dakota, headed for Montana's Yellowstone National Park. Why? Because something very dear to them was at risk. Bison were wandering out of Yellowstone and being killed.
>
> North America is the native home of bison, also called the American buffalo. Many years ago, bison were important to the Plains Indians. These Native Americans used all parts of the bison to survive. They were always careful not to waste anything. They ate the animals' meat and used their skins for clothing and shelter. Native Americans value and respect the animals they hunt.
>
> Others, sadly, don't feel that way. About 100 years ago, people had hunted so many bison that the great animal faced extinction. Now, the bison are at risk again, and many Native Americans are afraid. People are now hunting the last bison that roam free in the United States—the bison living in Yellowstone Park. Ranchers, mostly, support bison hunting. They're afraid the bison will give their cattle a disease. Ironically, there's no evidence that bison can give cattle this disease, yet the killing of bison continues.
>
> The Native Americans went on their walk to try to make people more aware. They hope, when people are aware, they'll help make the hunting stop, and that when the hunting stops, the great bison of Yellowstone will once again be allowed to roam free.
>
> **Explain who went on this walk, why they went, and what the walk was hoped to accomplish. Use information from the passage to support your answer.**

How would you go about answering this question? Keep the scoring tables on pages 250 and 251 in mind. On the next page is a sample answer.

Example of a Top-Scoring Response—5 Points
In February 1999, Native Americans from the Lakota tribe went on a 507-mile walk to Yellowstone National Park in Montana. They took this walk because people were hunting bison that wandered out of Yellowstone, and the bison are very important to the Lakota people. The bison are in danger of extinction. The Lakota respect animals deeply, especially the bison.

Though answers to questions like these can be much longer, an answer like this would receive a top score. Why? Because it answers all parts of the question in order, using information from the passage. If the author had left any part out, though, the score would have been lower. Complete, well-ordered answers score the best.

Example 1

They're older than nearly everything on Earth, and they're also extremely beautiful. They're dazzling and can seem fragile, but they're one of the hardest substances on Earth. What are these things that have so many contrasts? They're diamonds, of course. And they play many, many roles in our lives.

Most diamonds formed billions of years ago in an inner layer of the Earth called the mantle. The extreme heat of that layer—about 1,800 degrees Fahrenheit—forces dark black carbon into crystal-clear diamonds. While millions of years ago many diamonds shot from beneath the earth's surface in volcanic-type eruptions, today diamonds are mostly mined. Miners dig through about 250 tons of rock just to find one stone, and only a fraction of those stones are perfect enough to be used as jewels.

But there are many purposes for those less-than-perfect stones. Those that are too flawed can be used to create thousands of products: things like computer chips and protective eyeglasses. Because diamonds are so hard, they're great for cutting, grinding, and shaping building materials. Dentists even use them in their drills.

1   **How do diamonds form, how do we get them, and what roles do they play?**

_____

_____

_____

_____

_____

_____

_____

_____

_____

_____

_____

_____

_____

_____

_____

_____

_____

_____

 Discuss your answer with your teacher or class.

Lesson 38
Listening Skills

Your teacher will be reading you the story "The Elves and the Shoemaker." At the end of the story, you'll be asked to answer some questions. Before your teacher begins reading, review the following ways to listen carefully and take notes.

- Concentrate. Listening well takes work.
- Try to hear what's being said, not what you think you'll hear.
- Listen carefully for the main points.
- Take notes on the main points.

Note-Taking Skills

- Don't waste time writing every word. To save time, leave out simple words like "the" and "an."
- Use your own words as much as possible.
- Leave blank spaces between points. This way, you'll be able to find your information faster.
- Leave room in the margins for additional notes. You may want to add something you didn't hear the first time.
- Write largely enough and neatly enough so you can read your notes later.

Why does the shoemaker leave the shoe leather out the first night? How does he discover who's making the shoes? Write your answer on the lines below.

_____

_____

_____

Why do the shoemaker and his wife want to thank the elves? How do they do it? Write your answer on the lines below.

_____

_____

_____

What happens when the elves find what the shoemaker and his wife have left them? Why don't the elves return? Write your answer on the lines below.

_____

_____

_____

What is the theme of this story? How would the theme be different if the shoemaker and his wife never thanked the elves? Which events in the story would be different? Write your answer on the lines below.

Standards: S3.I.2.A Present (in essays, position papers, speeches, and debates) clear analyses of issues, ideas, texts, and experiences, supporting their positions with well-developed arguments.

Coached Listening

Your teacher will read you a letter to a newspaper editor. While reading, take notes on the selection. At the end of the selection, you will be asked to answer some questions in writing. Use your notes in your answers.

1 Who wrote the book the writer's daughter brought home?

_____

_____

_____

2 How does the main character act in the book?

_____

_____

_____

3 What is the letter writer's attitude towards Mrs. Wright?

_____

_____

_____

4   Why is the author opposed to this book? Use examples from the passage.

_____

_____

_____

_____

_____

5   What does the author suggest that the librarian do with the book?

_____

_____

_____

_____

_____

6 Rewrite this passage from the opposite point of view. Be sure to touch on all the same points and to use evidence to support your argument.

_____

_____

_____

_____

_____

_____

_____

_____

_____

_____

_____

_____

_____

_____

_____

_____

_____

_____

_____

_____

_____

_____

Test Practice

Read the following passage about Japanese warriors. Then do Numbers 1 through 3.

Samurai—The Japanese Warrior

A samurai is a traditional male Japanese warrior. He is famous for living according to an ethical code called "bushido," or "the way of the warrior." This code stresses loyalty, self-discipline, and respect.

More than 1,200 years ago, samurai were warriors who were hired to protect powerful landowners. Their main weapons were bows and arrows. They were highly trained, but they weren't necessarily soldiers for life. Between wars, they often worked on farms.

During the Era of Warring States, from 1467 to 1573, Japan's dozens of independent states were constantly at war. Samurai were in high demand, so they were increasingly important in society. From 1573 to 1603, though, Japan's states reunited. They also adopted a strict class system. Samurai could no longer be part-time farmers, and no one but samurai could carry swords. At this point, the sword was the samurai's main weapon.

After all these changes in Japan, the samurai's job started to change. First, being a samurai became a matter of birth. The children of samurai became samurai as well. This also meant that those children became members of the top social class. Samurai were the highest social class. But this class system had a drawback. Because samurai were now a class of people, instead of people who just fought for a living, they could not hire themselves out to the richest, most powerful landowners. Instead, they were expected to serve their local landowners for life.

By the mid-1800s, the Japanese government established a more modern military in which almost anyone could become a samurai, or soldier. As a result, the samurai class was no more. But samurai live on in legend, and some say that their code remains in the character and culture of the Japanese people.

1 This passage is an example of which of the following?

   A letter to the editor

   B textbook passage

   C newspaper article

   D book review

2 What was the function of the samurai in Japanese society?

_____

_____

_____

_____

_____

3 How did the position of the samurai change as Japan's states reunited?

_____

_____

_____

4 How did the role of the samurai change over time? Be sure to support your position with information from the passage.

_____

_____

_____

_____

_____

_____

_____

_____

_____

_____

_____

_____

_____

_____

_____

_____

_____

_____

3 Mechanics of Reading and Writing

GETTING THE IDEA

With the other units behind you, you've seen reading and writing from many different angles. In this unit, though, you'll get an up-close view.

You'll learn about simple and complex sentence types and how nouns and verbs relate. You'll also get a refresher on how sentences are punctuated. Then, you'll know the right spot for every comma, colon, and question mark.

Of course, you'll get to capitalize and spell correctly before you're through. And you'll have lots of practice and examples.

Standard: S1.1.2.F   Use standard English for formal presentation of information, selecting appropriate grammatical constructions and vocabulary, using a variety of sentence structures, and observing the rules of punctuation, capitalization, and spelling.

CHAPTER

9

Sentence Parts and Structure

Lesson 39: Types of Sentences

The sentence is the building block of writing, but what exactly is it? It's something that:

- begins with a capital letter
- ends with a period, a question mark, or an exclamation point
- expresses at least one thought
- has at least one subject and one predicate
- is either simple, compound, or complex

Simple Sentences

A **simple sentence** is the most basic kind. It expresses just one thought and has just one subject and just one predicate. The **subject** of the sentence is who or what the sentence is about. The **predicate** describes something the subject is or something it does.

But be careful: A subject doesn't have to be something you can see or touch. It can be an abstract idea, like hope or truth. "Unemployment rose in the second quarter" is a complete sentence. "Unemployment" is the subject. "Rose" is the predicate. But if a sentence doesn't have a subject and a predicate, it's not complete.

Example 1

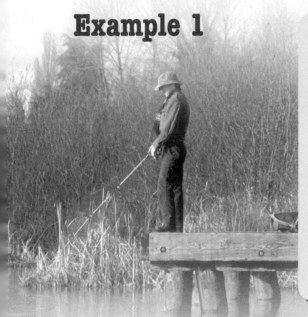

1 **Which of the following sentences is <u>not</u> complete?**

    A   He went fishing yesterday.

    B   Goldfish in the pond.

    C   Dinner was haddock.

    D   Onto his hook crept the bait.

 One of these sentences lacks either a subject or a predicate.

A **compound sentence** is, quite simply, two (or more) simple sentences put together. Once those ideas are part of one sentence, they're called **clauses**. Each clause must be **independent**, meaning it could be its own sentence. And while clauses must be independent, they should be related. A sentence like, "Robert scored two goals, and CDs cost too much" isn't proper form. But when two ideas are joined in one sentence word like "and" or "but" should connect them, or the clauses should be connected by a semicolon. These connecting words are called **conjunctions**.

Example 2

2 **Which of the following is a compound sentence?**

    A   Ty and Sally went to dinner.

    B   Ty wanted steak; Sally wanted grouper.

    C   Ty finished his steak and started eating Sally's dessert.

    D   Sally was furious.

 A compound sentence has two independent clauses that are connected.

Like compound sentences, complex sentences have two clauses—two parts with subjects and predicates. But in a **complex sentence**, one of the clauses is dependent, not independent. A **dependent clause**, also called a subordinate clause, doesn't express a complete thought. The dependent clause is underlined in the example below:

<u>After the girls went home</u>, Ginny cleaned the living room.

A dependent or subordinate clause often begins with a dependent marker, a word that makes it dependent on, or subordinate to, the other clause in the sentence. Words like "after," "although," and "when" are all dependent markers.

Example 3

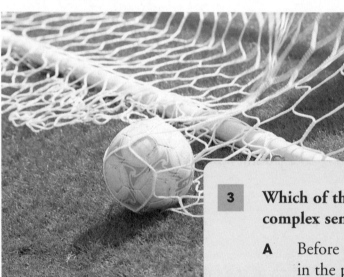

3 **Which of the following is an example of a complex sentence?**

A Before the match, they took a quick dip in the pool.

B Tess didn't like competing, but she did it anyway.

C Ken and I had both scored points; Dan and Robin both had saves.

D I knew I had done a good job, because the coach praised me later.

SELF Coach

Discuss your answer with your teacher or class.

Lesson 40
Noun-Verb Agreement

Noun-verb agreement simply means using the right verb for the subject. A singular subject, like *Steve* or *horse* takes a singular verb—panics or rises. Similarly, a plural subject—*camels* or *chestnuts*—take a plural verb—*spit* or *roast*.

Example 1

> **1** **In which sentence does the verb not agree with the subject?**
>
> **A** The dogs play virtually nonstop.
>
> **B** Honesty is now a rarity.
>
> **C** Tina and Marylou goes shopping together.
>
> **D** Sheets of ice cover the road.
>
>
>
> Remember that plural subjects take plural verbs.

Verb agreement can get tricky when you're not sure whether the subject is singular or plural. Once you know that, it's easy to pick the correct verb. Here are a few rules to help you avoid confusion:

- Don't be confused by words or phrases that appear between the subject and the verb.

  Example: The table under the trees is covered with a tablecloth.

- Pronouns like *each, everyone, everybody, anybody, anyone, none, nobody, neither, somebody,* and *someone* are singular. Remember to put singular forms of verbs after them.

  Example: Everyone parks by the grocery.

- Subjects joined by *and,* like *Mike and Joe, orange and blue,* and *he and I,* are plural.

  Example: Flour and water are the main ingredients.

- Plural words that have singular meanings, like *20 dollars, two-thirds,* and *37 pounds,* take singular verbs.

  Example: Twenty dollars is a huge tip.

- Even if a title of a work sounds plural, like *The Grapes of Wrath* does, it's always singular.

  Example: Johnny Mathis's "Greatest Hits" is worth buying.

When working with agreement, first find the subject. Then ask yourself if it's singular or plural. After that, it should be easy to pick the right verb for the job.

Example 2

2 **In which sentence does the verb not agree with the subject?**

A Everybody wanted to see the polo match.

B Five dollars did not seem like much to lose.

C The vice president and her assistant are meeting now.

D Honor among thieves are in decline.

Discuss your answer with your teacher or class.

Grammar Practice

Read the following passage about a young boy. Then answer the questions that follow.

Raoul woke with a start. The TV blared a car commercial into the darkened room. "Commercials like that is such a nuisance," he thought groggily. Then he realized it. He must have fallen asleep, because he wasn't in his bed. He was on the couch. And everyone were gone.

"What time was it?" he wondered. "Where was Uncle Sal?" Uncle Sal's chair was empty, and his dessert plate was abandoned. Leaning toward the bathroom, Raoul asked, "Uncle Sal? You in there?" No response. Starting to sweat a little, he pushed himself off the couch. "Uncle Sal!" Then, he saw the open door. "Oh, no," he muttered. "Barbara's gonna kill me." He checked the garage and the driveway. Sure enough, the old Lincoln Continental was gone. Where had Uncle Sal gone?

Raoul sat next to the phone as he prepared to call his sister. He wracks his brain for things to tell her. But what? What nonsense had Uncle Sal been talking earlier? Something about seeing his brother, Johnny? Johnny had been dead for years, Raoul thought. Maybe his uncle had lost touch with reality and for good.

1 It is in correct noun-verb agreement to say which of the following?

A Starting to sweat a little, he pushed himself off the couch.

B He wracks his brain for things to tell her.

C He must have fallen asleep, because he wasn't in his bed.

D Sure enough, the old Lincoln Continental was gone.

2 Which of the following is a complex sentence?

F Raoul sat next to the phone, as he prepared to call his sister.

G The TV blared a car commercial into the darkened room.

H No response.

J Raoul woke with a start.

3 Which of the following is a compound sentence?

A Something about seeing his brother, Johnny?

B What nonsense had Uncle Sal been talking earlier?

C "Where was Uncle Sal?"

D Uncle Sal's chair was empty, and his dessert plate was abandoned.

4 How would you rewrite this paragraph with only simple and compound sentences? Write your answer on the lines below.

_____

_____

_____

_____

_____

_____

_____

_____

_____

_____

_____

_____

_____

_____

_____

_____

_____

_____

_____

_____

Read the following passage about a trip to London. Then do Numbers 5 through 8.

My family travels a lot. We've been on trips to the Grand Canyon, and we've been to Montreal. Each were terrific in its own way, but one was the best. It was a trip my family and I took to London when I was 10.

London is a great place to visit, because it seems quite different from America. They still speaks English, though, so you don't have to learn another language. The first thing I noticed about London was how green it was. You always hear about how rainy London is, but you never hear about the parks and gardens. The parks and gardens are spectacular. All that rain is great for flowers, and warm temperatures is, too. My favorite was the rose garden in Regent's Park.

If you're at all interested in kings, queens, and castles, London is the place for you. We watched the changing of the guard at Buckingham Palace, and we went to see the royal jewels at the Tower of London. At another palace, Hampton Court, we wandered in a huge maze made of bushes. We also had tea there. Tea isn't just a hot drink, it's a meal of scones and jam, little sandwiches, and even cakes. It's my new favorite meal!

5 Which of the following is not a complex sentence?

F If you're at all interested in kings, queens, and castles, London is the place for you.

G London is a great place to visit, because it seems quite different from America.

H We watched the changing of the guard at Buckingham Palace, and we went to see the royal jewels at the Tower of London.

J Each were terrific in its own way, but one was the best.

6 Which of the following has proper noun-verb agreement?

A All that rain is great for flowers, and warm temperatures is, too.

B They still speaks English, though, so you don't have to learn another language.

C Each were terrific in its own way, but one was the best.

D Tea isn't just a hot drink, it's a meal of scones and jam, little sandwiches, and even cakes.

7 Which of the following is not a simple sentence?

F My favorite was the rose garden in Regent's Park.

G My family travels a lot.

H Each were terrific in its own way, but one was the best.

J It's my new favorite meal!

8 What are some examples of compound sentences in the passage? Give two or three examples.

_____

_____

_____

_____

_____

_____

Standard: S1.I.2.F Use standard English for formal presentation of information, selecting appropriate grammatical constructions and vocabulary, using a variety of sentence structures, and observing the rules of punctuation, capitalization, and spelling.

CHAPTER 10

Punctuation

Lesson 41: Punctuation: Colons and Semicolons

You're probably pretty familiar with periods. They mark the ends of sentences. Pretty easy, right? Well, the punctuation you find within and between sentences is a little more complicated. Let's review two examples of that type of punctuation: colons and semicolons.

Colons

Colons introduce things. They say to the reader, "Pay attention! Something important's coming here." Usually, what comes after the colon is an explanation of what came before the colon or gives additional information. Consider these examples:

> They have three daughters: Amy, Kate, and Sady.

> There's only one thing you should know about Judy: She loves her family.

Colons used after a greeting in a business letter do the same thing. They introduce what comes next. Here are some examples:

> Dear Sir or Madam:

> To Whom It May Concern:

A common use of the colon, though, is separating the hour from the minutes in expressions of time-or minutes from seconds, as in these examples:

> The plane is due in at 12:43 PM.

> The Swedish champion came in first at 2:04:21.

Example 1

1 **Which example does <u>not</u> show the correct use of the colon?**

A His speech isn't scheduled until 7:30 PM.

B Dear Mom: Camp is great.

C My friend: Mary is the best friend you could have.

D Recess starts at 12:00 PM.

QUICK Coach

Colons are generally used to help show time or introduce things.

Semicolons

If a comma is a pause, a semicolon is a double pause. Semicolons are used mostly for two reasons:

- to join two independent clauses without a conjunction (like "John wrote; I painted.")
- to separate items in a list when some or all of the items include commas ("Max was good at science, math, and art; pretty good at English and French; and pretty lousy at history, Spanish, and civics.")

The first use is far more common; it's the one you should focus on. Here are some examples of how to correctly use the semicolon to connect two independent clauses:

The game was in a rain delay; I watched anyway.

James started to listen to opera; Jennifer couldn't stand it.

Everybody cheered for Rachel; she bowed deeply.

Remember, there should be no conjunction where these two independent clauses meet. Don't write "The game was in a rain delay; but I watched anyway." The semicolon does the work of both the comma and the conjunction.

Example 2

2 **Which of the following sentences needs a semicolon?**

A Jen and Sue went to lunch.

B David rode his horse; I rode mine.

C Michelle married Don, and Marcie married Peter.

D The clock had stopped the game was over.

Discuss your answer with your teacher or class.

Lesson 42
Punctuation: Commas

There are many uses for **commas**, which generally add pause in sentences. Commas are most often used for these purposes:

- to separate three or more items in a series (like "blue, red, and purple")
- to set off a direct quotation (as in "She said, 'Make me!'")
- before a conjunction when linking two independent clauses (like "We were hungry, so we ate.")

Here are some examples of the correct use of commas:

Bananas, apples, and cherries can all be very sweet.

Brandon laughed and said, "You got me."

They watched him leave, but he didn't look back.

Example 1

1 **Which sentence is missing a comma?**

A Our favorite game is "Tic, Tac, Toe."

B Ted yelled, "That's not nice!"

C We didn't know what to do so we did nothing.

D When it was time, we got up to leave.

Discuss your answer with your teacher or class.

NOTICE: Photocopying any part of this book is forbidden by law.

279

Standards: S1.1.2.F Use standard English for formal presentation of information, selecting appropriate grammatical constructions and vocabulary, using a variety of sentence structures, and observing the rules of punctuation, capitalization, and spelling.

Lesson 43
Punctuation: Ending Marks

Periods are probably the most common punctuation mark. They come at the end of the sentence to show where it stops. They also appear after abbreviations, as in "Mr. Smith Goes to Washington."

Here are some examples of periods used correctly:

Mrs. Pirozzi arrived early.

On Tuesday, Tricia went to see Dr. Serrano.

Hamburgers are better with ketchup.

Occasionally, sentences end with different marks. When a sentence is a question, for example, it should end with a **question mark**, as in "What was that?" When the sentence expresses strong emotion, like excitement, it should end with an **exclamation point** as in "That was an earthquake!" Otherwise, every sentence should end with a period.

Example 1

1 **Which sentence uses the period correctly?**

A Wait. until later for lunch.

B Mr. Roberts will be back soon.

C "Not this time." he said.

D Look. that way, to the beach

Periods should appear in the middle of sentences only when they are used for abbreviations.

Example 2

2 **Which sentence is punctuated correctly?**

A "I'm so excited?" she yelled.

B "Hey, stop that man!" he cried.

C "Where's the bus stop!" she asked.

D "Yes, that's the right way?" he said.

Discuss your answer with your teacher or class.

Grammar Practice

Read the following passage, which is from a Native American tale. Then do Numbers 1 through 4.

How Indian Summer Came to Be

From an Abenaki folk tale

Long; long ago there was a good man named Notki who worked hard to provide for his family. He cultivated his gardens every year: to be sure there would be plenty of food. He always gave thanks each harvest to Tabal, the Master, of Life?

Then, one year, there was a late frost; and his crops died from the cold. Undeterred, he planted again, but then there was a drought, and his crops died of thirst. He planted a third time; but it was so late in the season that the cold weather of early winter killed his plants. Notki was very troubled; he was getting worried. Although his wife and children had gathered some foods from the forest; it would not be enough to see them through the winter. One autumn night. he made a small fire and offered tobacco to Tabal and asked him for help so that he could see his family through the coming cold time. Then he went to sleep, and he dreamed. In his dream, Tabaldak came to him telling him, "I give you these special seeds, and a time in which to plant them, Notki."

1 Which of the following sentences uses commas correctly?

A Tabal came to him telling him, "I give you these special seeds, and a time in which to plant them, Notki."

B Long; long ago there was a good man named Notki who worked hard to provide for his family.

C Undeterred, he planted again, but then there was a drought, and his crops died of thirst.

D He always gave thanks each harvest to Tabal, the Master, of Life?

2 Read the following sentence from the passage:

He cultivated his gardens every year: to be sure there would be plenty of food.

How would you rewrite this sentence to use the colon correctly?

F He cultivated his gardens every year: He wanted to be sure there would be plenty of food.

G He cultivated his gardens every year to be sure: there would be plenty of food.

H He cultivated his gardens: every year: to be sure there would be plenty of food.

J He cultivated his gardens every year to be sure there would be: plenty of food.

3 Which of the following sentences uses semicolons correctly?

A Long; long ago there was a good man named Notki who worked hard to provide for his family.

B He planted a third time; but it was so late in the season that the autumn cold killed his plants.

C Notkikad was very troubled; he was getting worried.

D Although his wife and children had gathered some foods from the forest; it would not be enough to see them through the winter.

NOTICE: Photocopying any part of this book is forbidden by law.

283

4 How would you rewrite this passage using different kinds of ending punctuation, including exclamation points and question marks? Make sure to correct all errors. Write your answer on the lines below.

_____

_____

_____

_____

_____

_____

_____

_____

_____

_____

_____

_____

_____

_____

_____

_____

_____

_____

_____

_____

> **Read the beginning of this famous old story. Then do Numbers 5 through 8.**

From "The Princess and the Pea"

by Hans Christian Anderson

Once upon a time; there was a prince who wanted to marry a real princess. To this end, he traveled the globe, seeking a true princess, but to no avail? No matter how many times he met women claiming to be princesses, he was never completely sure that they were. There was always something that did not seem quite right about them. They seemed odd. Finally, he gave up and went back home, sadly He had wished so much that he would find a real princess.

Soon after he returned, there was a terrible storm one night. Lightning flashes lit the sky like daylight. The thunder boomed so deeply that it rattled the castle, and the rain came down in buckets. Then a quiet tapping was heard at the town gate. The prince's father, the old king, went out to open it; he was surprised to see a young woman, drenched to the bone! The poor young woman looked a mess. Her hair was flattened and dripping with water. Her clothes; heavy with rain; hung from her body like a scarecrow's. Her skin looked pale from the cold, and she was shivering horribly. Yet; despite her appearance, she claimed to be a princess!

5 Which of the following uses end punctuation correctly?

F Yet; despite her appearance, she claimed to be a princess!

G There was always something that did not seem quite right about them. Finally, he gave up and went back home, sadly

H To this end, he circumnavigated the globe, seeking a true princess, but to no avail?

J Then a quiet tapping was heard at the town gate.

6 Which of the following does <u>not</u> use semicolons correctly?

A Her clothes; heavy with rain; hung from her body like a scarecrow's.

B Yet; despite her appearance, she claimed to be a princess!

C Once upon a time; there was a prince who wanted to marry a real princess.

D The prince's father, the old king, went out to open it; he was surprised to see a young woman, drenched to the bone!

7 Read the following sentences from the passage:

There was always something that did not seem quite right about them. They seemed odd.

What is the correct way to use a colon in these sentences?

F There was always something that did not seem quite right about them: They seemed odd.

G There was always something: that did not seem quite right about them. They seemed odd.

H There was always something that did not seem quite right about them. They seemed: odd.

J There was always something that did not seem quite: right about them. They seemed odd.

8 How would you use commas correctly in this passage? Use two or three examples.

_____

_____

_____

_____

_____

_____

CHAPTER 11

Capitalization and Spelling

Lesson 44: Capitalization

Using capital letters in the correct places is called **capitalization**. This is another way to make writing clearer. Capital letters help us immediately identify where new sentences begin. They also help you spot names right away.

Always remember to capitalize:

- words that begin sentences
- proper names of people (like Alfred Hitchcock and Ghandi), organizations and institutions (like the Frick Collection and Amnesty International), and places (like the Grand Canyon, Manhattan, and Asia)
- months and days (like September and Saturday)
- historical events (like the Civil War and World War II)
- languages (like French and Polish)
- brands (like Quaker State and General Mills)
- titles before names (like Dr. Burack and Professor Lynch)
- words that begin or end titles (like "The Pirates of the Caribbean")
- other important words in titles (like "The Best Years of Our Lives")
- the pronoun "I"

And here are some examples of properly capitalized sentences:

I brought Virginia a Band-Aid Friday when she scraped her knees.

Amy is going with Dr. Franklin to the Kennedy Center in April.

"Paul Revere's Ride" takes place during the American Revolution.

Example 1

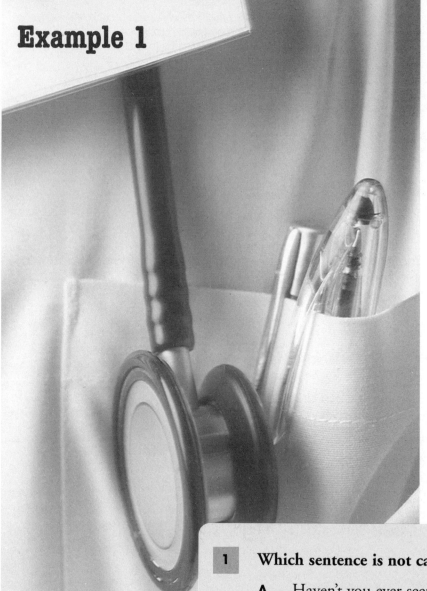

1 **Which sentence is not capitalized properly?**

A Haven't you ever seen "One More Time to Go?"

B I know French, but English is my first language.

C My Doctor, Les Boone, wants to take some tests.

D I need to brush up on World War I.

SELF Coach Discuss your answer with your teacher or class.

Lesson 45
Spelling

For some, spelling in English can be frustrating. Different letters can make the same sound, as in "here" and "hear." Sometimes, the same letters can make different sounds, as with "ou" in "bought," "bounce," and "tour." And what about the silent "e"? Or the fact that "bough" rhymes with "cow" but "tough" rhymes with "guff"? It can certainly be confusing.

English spelling is so crazy that mostly we learn to spell it just by practicing reading and writing, and memorizing lists of the correct spelling of words. There are, however, some general rules you can follow:

- Write "i" before "e."

  Examples: fiery, fiend, friend, mischief, view, believe

- But do not write "i" before "e" after "c" or when sounding like a long "a" as in "neighbor" and "weigh."

  Examples: receive, deceive, reign (one notable exception: weird, where there is no c and no "a" sound—just remember, it's weird)

- When a word ends with a silent "e," drop the "e" when adding a suffix beginning with a vowel.

  Examples: skate-skating, like-likable

- Don't drop the "e" when the suffix begins with a consonant.

  Examples: state-statement, use-useful

- When "y" is the last letter in a word and the "y" follows a consonant, change the "y" to "i" before adding any suffix, except those beginning in "i."

  Examples: beauty-beautiful, beautify; hurry-hurries, hurried (but hurrying)

- When "y" is the last letter in a word and the "y" follows a vowel, then you can simply add the suffix without changing anything.

  Examples: toy-toys, toyed; play-plays, played

- When a one-syllable word ends in a consonant after one vowel, double the final consonant before adding a suffix that begins with a vowel.

  Examples: bat-batting, batted, batter; hop-hopping, hopped

- If the word has more than one syllable, but the accent or emphasis is on the final syllable, the same rule applies: Double the final consonant.

  Examples: control-controlled, controlling; prefer-preferring, preferred.

Of course, a spell-check on your computer will help with a lot of spelling problems. But you don't have spell-check when you take a test. Also, spell-checking will miss many words that are misspelled because they are **homophones**, that is, words that sound alike but are spelled differently. Homophones are some of the most commonly misspelled words.

Example 1

1 **Which word in the following sentence is misspelled?**

We weren't jealous because, rightfully, it was there turn.

A jealous

B rightfully

C because

D there

Discuss your answer with your teacher or class.

Grammar Practice

Read the following passage from a newspaper. Then do Numbers 1 and 2.

VOTERS INDECIDED IN UPCOMING MAYORAL RACE

PRETTYVILLE, IN—The race is quickly coming down to the wire. Both candidates in Tuesday's election present their platforms as the answer to Prettyville's problems. polls show the townspeople are as yet undecided about whether to vote for the incumbent, Joe N. Charge, or his challenger, Samantha D. Bater. Supporters for both sides express enthusiasm and confidence in their candidates.

1 Which of the following sentences has a capitalization error?

A The race is quickly coming down to the wire.

B Supporters for both sides express enthusiasm and confidence in their candidates.

C polls show the townspeople are as yet undecided about whether to vote for the incumbent, Joe N. Charge, or his challenger, Samantha D. Bater.

D Both candidates in Tuesday's election present their platforms as the answer to Prettyville's problems.

2 How would you rewrite the headline using proper capitalization? Write your answer on the lines below.

_____

_____

_____

Read the following passage about the circus. Then do Numbers 3 and 4.

All year long, doreen had been looking forward to going to the circus. She loved to watch the Trapeze Artists go soaring through the air and the brave lion tamers showing off their trained animals. She always laughed whenever the clowns came out, and a shiver would run up her spine whenever the Ringmaster made an announcement in his deep, booming voice. It was the night before the circus, and Doreen was supposed to be sleeping. She heard her Parents talking in the kitchen.

"Isn't there anything we can do?" she heard her Mother ask. "No," her father replied. "Doreen has her heart set on going to the circus."

3 Which of the following is capitalized correctly?

F *She heard her Parents talking in the kitchen.*

G *All yeer long, doreen had been looking forward to going to the circus.*

H *It was the night before the circus, and Doreen was supposed to be sleeping.*

J *She loved to watch the Trapeze Artists go soreing through the air.*

4 How would you rewrite the passage to fix all capitalization mistakes? Write your answer on the lines below.

_____

_____

_____

_____

_____

_____

_____

_____

_____

_____

_____

_____

_____

_____

_____

_____

_____

_____

_____

POSTTEST

English
Language Arts
BOOK 1

Session 1

Reading

D*irections*
The following magazine article describes an exhibit by an artist named Rembrandt. Read "Rembrandt Exhibit Spotlights Artist's Life." Then do Numbers 1 through 5.

Rembrandt Exhibit

Spotlights Artist's Life

by Dawn MacDougal

Like his art, now on display at the Johnsonville Art Museum, Rembrandt was full of shadows and light. But, as many know, his once-bright life eventually descended into darkness. When did the light give way to shadows—and why? Who was this man who touched so many people with his paintings?

Early Talent, Early Fame

Born in Holland, Rembrandt embraced painting at a tender age. It was clear, very early, where his talent lay. His earliest subjects were glossy, vivid, colorful portrayals. His subjects? Events from history and the Bible.

At 15, he traveled to Amsterdam to study his art. He would leave home more than once. Longing for home, though, he didn't stay away long. Once he returned, he quickly, and justifiably, achieved local fame.

Fame Grows and Multiplies

Eventually, back in Holland, Rembrandt began to teach art. Among his students, like his audiences, he was well-respected.

Again, though, he felt the pull of that distant city, Amsterdam. So, in 1632, he made the move again. This time, though, the move would prove more permanent. Once he settled in, he began painting the portraits of many of Amsterdam's well-known people. It wasn't long before this work, too, was winning fame.

Rembrandt was soon to find success in other ways, too. In 1634, he fell in love with and married a woman named Saskia. Wealthy and educated, she served as a model for many of his paintings. Life, for a while, went well for Rembrandt. He was a successful painter, he was happily married, and he started having children. He and Saskia even moved into a large home where he hung many of his paintings—his own as well as those he had collected from other painters.

Life Takes a Bad Turn

Then tragedy struck, again and again. At early ages, three of Rembrandt's four children died. Then, in 1642, he lost Saskia, too.

Rembrandt—and his work—was never the same again. Once vivid and bright, his paintings began to take on dark, somber tones. Dark colors surrounded the painting's figures, but the figures themselves were painted as if under soft lights. Somehow, Rembrandt used his despair to make his paintings even more beautiful. He painted one of his most famous pieces, "The Night Watch," during this time.

Soon, it became clear the Rembrandt was painting more and more for himself—and less and less for other people. While his paintings were still beautiful, still brilliant, fewer and fewer people bought them. It was nothing like the old days. Unable to make enough from painting, Rembrandt was eventually forced to sell his house. By 1657, his house and belongings had been auctioned off, and he was bankrupt. It was wildly dichotomous from the place he had been a few years ago.

Painting Goes On, and On, and On

Rembrandt never stopped painting, though. Until he died in 1669, he continued to paint, and paint, and paint. Some say it's the only thing that kept him alive, especially after all he had lost. Rembrandt's career had accumulated a wealth of art—over 600 paintings, 300 etchings, and 1,400 drawings. Among the most fascinating were the pictures he painted of himself.

Rembrandt's gone now, so we'll never know more about this great artist. But he's left an incredible legacy of craftsmanship, one that records the incredible lifetime of an irreplaceable natural talent.

Editorial research by Cassie David

Go On

1 Read this sentence from the passage.

> **It was wildly dichotomous from the place where he had come.**

In this sentence, "dichotomous" means

A effective

B disturbing

C different

D beautiful

2 All of the following is true of Rembrandt's early life **except**

F his house was auctioned off by 1657

G he was born in Holland

H he traveled to Amsterdam at 15

J his early works were of religious subjects

3 Why did Rembrandt's painting suddenly change?

A Some unfortunate events made him very sad.

B He grew tired of painting the same thing.

C Saskia refused to be in the paintings anymore.

D His children were hurting his concentration.

4 Rembrandt's paintings were probably

F best in the beginning

G more popular when they were colorful

H only about one thing

J about Rembrandt's life

5 Rembrandt would probably agree with which of the following statements?

A Life affects how you paint.

B You should only paint when you are happy.

C Painting is more important than family.

D You should only paint to make money.

Session 1

*D*irections
Read the following poem about a bird's nest. Then do Numbers 6 through 10.

The Snow-Filled Nest
by Rose Terry Cooke

It swings upon the leafless tree,
By stormy winds blown to and fro;
Deserted, lonely, sad to see,
    And full of cruel snow.

In summer's noon the leaves above
Made dewy shelter from the heat;
The nest was full of life and love;
    Ah, life and love are sweet!

The tender brooding of the day,
The silent, peaceful dreams of night,
The joys that patience overpay,
    The cry of young delight,

The song that through the branches rings,
The nestling crowd with eager eyes,
The flutter soft of untried wings.
    The flight of glad surprise.

All, all are gone! I know not where;
And still upon the cold gray tree,
Lonely, and tossed by every air,
    That snow-filled nest I see.

I, too, had once a place of rest,
Where life, and love, and peace were mine,
Even as the wild-birds build their nest,
    When skies and summer shine.

But winter came, the leaves were dead;
The mother-bird was first to go,
The nestlings from my sight have fled;
    The nest is full of snow.

Go On

6 The **theme** of this poem is

F summertime is birds' best time

G happiness is temporary

H empty nests should hold snow

J plant trees in the wintertime

7 Read this sentence from the passage.

The nestling crowd with eager eyes.

In this sentence, the word "nestling" means

A leaf

B branch

C light

D baby bird

8 The author of this poem probably feels that

F trees look their worst in winter

G birds are an unimportant part of nature

H nests should not be seen in trees

J loneliness is an unpleasant part of life

9 What is the snow-filled nest a symbol of?

A emptiness

B young birds

C gray trees

D happiness

10 What is the setting of this passage?

F summer

G winter

H a zoo

J a bird bath

*D*irections

Read the article "Life on Earth—and Mars?" about the possibilities for life in outer space. Then do Numbers 11 through 15.

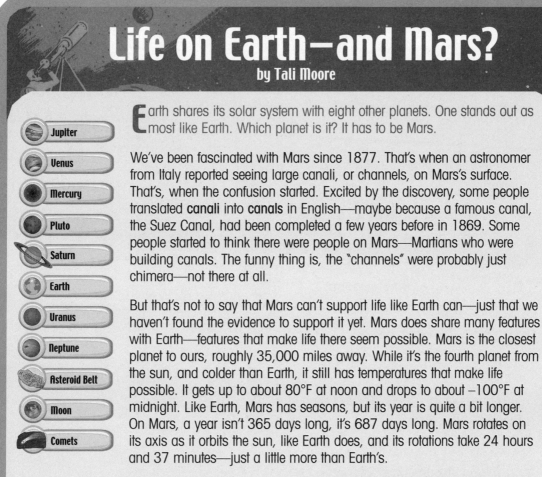

Life on Earth—and Mars?
by Tali Moore

Jupiter

Venus

Mercury

Pluto

Saturn

Earth

Uranus

Neptune

Asteroid Belt

Moon

Comets

Earth shares its solar system with eight other planets. One stands out as most like Earth. Which planet is it? It has to be Mars.

We've been fascinated with Mars since 1877. That's when an astronomer from Italy reported seeing large canali, or channels, on Mars's surface. That's when the confusion started. Excited by the discovery, some people translated **canali** into **canals** in English—maybe because a famous canal, the Suez Canal, had been completed a few years before in 1869. Some people started to think there were people on Mars—Martians who were building canals. The funny thing is, the "channels" were probably just chimera—not there at all.

But that's not to say that Mars can't support life like Earth can—just that we haven't found the evidence to support it yet. Mars does share many features with Earth—features that make life there seem possible. Mars is the closest planet to ours, roughly 35,000 miles away. While it's the fourth planet from the sun, and colder than Earth, it still has temperatures that make life possible. It gets up to about 80°F at noon and drops to about −100°F at midnight. Like Earth, Mars has seasons, but its year is quite a bit longer. On Mars, a year isn't 365 days long, it's 687 days long. Mars rotates on its axis as it orbits the sun, like Earth does, and its rotations take 24 hours and 37 minutes—just a little more than Earth's.

As similar as Mars is to Earth, does it have the one thing it needs to support life: water? No. So far, no water has been found on Mars. Space probes from Earth have discovered that most of Mars's surface is a vast desert—a dull red or orange desert with huge volcanoes, a giant canyon, and lava plains. But that doesn't mean there was never any water on Mars or that there isn't any underground. Mars has polar caps that seem to contain water, ice, and frozen carbon dioxide (the main component of its atmosphere). There is evidence, too, that floods and small rivers have caused erosion. Some 2 to 4 billion years ago, when Mars was warmer, there may have been large lakes or oceans.

That there was water in Mars's past means there may have once been life there, too. So far, though, no evidence has been found. Unmanned spacecraft have landed on the red planet and returned with photos and soil samples. Scientists have studied the photos and soil samples at length, searching for microorganisms or other signs of life. None, unfortunately, have ever been found. The scientists' mission, though, is worthwhile.

Go On

11 This passage is mainly intended to

A   discuss whether or not there could be life on Mars

B   tell an exciting outer space adventure story

C   explain the possibilities of space travel

D   tell what an interesting place Mars is

12 Which of the following is an opinion?

F   Mars is the closest planet to Earth.

G   Two moons orbit Mars.

H   It gets up to 80°F at noon on Mars.

J   The scientists' mission, though, is worthwhile.

13 Why do scientists believe that there may be water on Mars?

A   because they have found evidence, such as polar caps

B   because other scientists believe it

C   because they have hope for life in outer space

D   because they know more than we do about the planets

14 Which of the following is a difference between Earth and Mars?

F   Mars is the closest planet to Earth.

G   The day on the planets is about 24 hours long.

H   Mars has no water.

J   The temperatures on Mars could support life.

15 Read the following sentence from the passage.

The 'channels' were probably just chimeras—not there at all.

In this sentence, what does the word "chimeras" mean?

A   chilly

B   contained

C   illusions

D   vessels

Session 1

***D**irections*
**Read this myth about a girl with a remarkable talent. Then do Numbers
16 through 20.**

ATALANTA
AND HER SUITOR

by Thomas Shue

Atalanta was the daughter of the King of Beotia. They called her "Atalanta of the Swift Foot," because she could run very fast. She vowed to the gods to marry only a young man who could outrun her. Now, Atalanta was very fair—Many young men wanted to marry her. Eventually, there were so many young men clamoring for her that the king made a law: Any man who raced Atalanta and lost would also lose his life.

Once a young man named Hippomenes came into the country. He followed the crowd of people to the course where Atalanta and her suitors would be racing. Watching the men prepare for the race, he heard the folk say, "Poor men. As mighty and as high spirited as they look, by sunset their lives will be gone, for Atalanta will run past them as she has run past all the others. That's why she wears the black heart on her chest." Then Hippomenes saw Atalanta. Over her bare shoulders her hair streamed, blown backward by the wind that met her flight. Her fair neck shone, and her little feet were like flying doves. Fire glowed inside her, despite the black heart pinned on her. On and on she went, as swift as an arrow shot from a bow. As he watched the race, his heart was set upon winning her for his bride.

Go On

After the race, Hippomenes watched Atalanta, who was standing with her father as he pronounced doom on her latest unlucky suitors. Hippomenes went up to them and challenged Atalanta to a race. Atalanta was as kind as she was swift. She regretted the deaths of the men who tried to win her hand, even though they agreed to the risk. Her heart went out to the young man before her, so she begged him not to race her. "Don't speak of it," she said. "You risk your life, and I'm not worthy of the price." Hippomenes replied that without her his life was useless. The old king sighed and told Hippomenes he could race Atalanta, alone, the next day.

As father and daughter left, Hippomenes stood and watched the sandy course where he would soon meet his fate. Soon, he saw Aphrodite, the goddess of love, walking toward him. She said, "Hippomenes, you are a worthy young man, and I would like to see you win this race. I would also like to see Atalanta married. So here—take these." With that, she held up three golden apples that dazzled his eyes. "Put them in your pockets, and tomorrow as you race, you will know how they can help you."

From the first steps of the race, Hippomenes and Atalanta skimmed the sandy course like swallows. But it was clear that Atalanta was far faster. As hard as he tried, Atalanta drew farther and farther ahead. Then he remembered the golden apples. He took one from his pocket and threw it on the course ahead of her. When she stooped to pick it up, he passed her, taking the lead for a few minutes before she caught him again. When he felt himself falling too far behind, he threw another, and this time the apple rolled off the course. Atalanta went after it, and Hippomenes took the lead again. She passed him once more and soon neared the finish line. He was exhausted. Hippomenes gathered what was left of his courage and strength and threw the third apple. It bounced off the course, and she followed it, righting herself just in time to cross the finish line . . . a few steps behind Hippomenes.

When Hippomenes returned to his faraway home, it was with a beautiful new bride, a wedding gift of horses, and the three golden apples of Aphrodite.

16 Hippomenes attained his goal through

    F fast running

    G assistance from the gods at the last minute

    H shrewd use of the apples

    J overpowering Atalanta

17 The story is probably intended to show that

    A winning is the most important thing

    B it is best to be kind and do the right thing

    C competition is the only way to show who's right

    D love is more important than competition

18 Why does the author compare Atalanta to an arrow?

    F to show what she looks like

    G to tell readers about arrows

    H to describe life in ancient times

    J to show how fast she ran

19 The author says of Atalanta that "fire glowed inside her" to make readers feel

    A scared of her

    B interested in her

    C bored by her

    D angry at her

20 Atalanta's black heart in this story represents

    F her bad mood

    G her sadness

    H her family

    J her black hair

Go On

Directions

Read this essay about camouflage. Then do Numbers 21 through 25.

CAN YOU SEE ME NOW?

by Bedelia Miller

Now you see that animal—and now you don't. Amazing feats of invisibility are found everywhere in nature. What are those feats called? Camouflage.

Most animals have developed a natural form of camouflage that helps them either find food or avoid becoming food for other animals. The most common kind is called general resemblance. In this kind of camouflage, animals use color to blend in with their habitats. Deer, squirrels, and hedgehogs, for example, are all a brownish color that matches the brown of the trees and soil in a forest. Sharks, dolphins, and many other sea animals have a grayish-blue coloring that helps them blend in with the soft light under water.

Almost all animals blend in with their habitats to some degree. Very few, though, manage to use adaptive camouflage. An animal's habitat can change from time to time— namely when the seasons change. In the spring and summer, an animal's habitat might be full of greens and browns, but in the winter everything might be white because it's covered with snow. Many birds and mammals actually produce different colors of feathers or fur depending on the season. The Arctic fox, for instance, is brown in the summer but white in the winter.

Session 1

Other animals need new camouflage when they migrate to new places. Many fish species release hormones that change the coloring of their scales to match the changing scenery. Others change the coloring of their skin by changing their diets. When a nudibranch, a type of mollusk that lives in the sea, eats a particular type of coral, its body deposits the pigments from that coral in its skin. The skin then takes on the color of the mollusk's home.

Some animals use special resemblance to appear to be something other than what they are. They use special resemblance as a tool, not to blend in, but to cloak themselves. The walking stick, for example, is an insect that looks like an ordinary twig. Katydids are insects that look just like tree leaves. The back of a hawk moth caterpillar is designed not just to fool a predator but to scare it away: It looks like a snake head. Another form of disguise involves bright patterns that keep a predator from getting a clear sense of where an animal begins and ends. The stripes on a herd of zebras may seem to make them stand out, but they actually present a confusing zigzag of lines to a lion, making it hard for the lion to stalk and attack one animal.

What about humans? Humans with specialized jobs use both general and special resemblance. Soldiers wear camouflage fatigues that mimic the coloration of the land where they're stationed. So do hunters, who wear earth-toned clothes with dark, branchlike stripes to resemble the forest. On the other hand, spies use special resemblance, changing their appearances not to blend into their backgrounds but to make them look like other people. Even those of us who aren't trying to hunt or keep from being hunted use camouflage every now and then. The clothes we choose can increase or decrease the amount we stand out in our environments. What, for instance, would a shy young man wear on his first day at a new school? Most likely, jeans, a T-shirt, and sneakers, like everyone else.

Go On

21 How does the author organize the essay?

   A by comparing two kinds of animals

   B by stating a main idea and then giving examples

   C by giving an argument and defending it

   D by separating it into sections

22 It is likely that people who use camouflage

   F use it just like animals

   G only use it for evil purposes

   H can only use it in certain environments

   J do not enjoy using it

23 According to the article, the Arctic fox

   A deposits pigments in its fur

   B releases hormones that change its fur color

   C is brown in the summer but white in the winter

   D scares other animals away with its fur

24 What is probably the author's opinion about camouflage?

   F Camouflage is a unique and interesting feat of nature.

   G Animals who use camouflage are smarter than other animals.

   H Camouflage really only has one purpose.

   J People who use camouflage have better survival skills.

25 Why would someone dress like everyone else on the first day of school?

   A so that he or she didn't stand out

   B so that he or she could hide

   C so that everyone would notice him or her

   D as a way of being funny

26 Why do hunters try to resemble the forest that surrounds them?

   F because they like the colors

   G because it helps them find animals

   H because the animals are drawn to them

   J because it helps them sneak up on animals

STOP

English Language Arts
BOOK 2

This test asks you to write about what you have listened to or read. Your writing will NOT be scored on your personal opinions. It WILL be scored on:

- how clearly you organize and express your ideas
- how accurately and completely you answer the questions
- how well you support your ideas with examples
- how interesting and enjoyable your writing is
- how correctly you use grammar, spelling, punctuation, and paragraphs

Whenever you see this symbol, be sure to plan and check your writing.

Session 2

Listening

*D*irections

In this part of the test, you will listen to a story called "Old Joe and the Carpenter." Then you will answer some questions to show how well you understood what was read.

You will listen to the article twice. As you listen carefully, you may take notes on the articles any time you wish during the readings. You may use these notes to answer the questions that follow. Use the space on Pages 312 and 313 for your notes.

This article is about two farmers and a carpenter, one of whom does something unexpected and changes the outcome of the story. This story started as a folk tale in the United States. Here are the spellings of some words that may be unfamiliar to you:

- spouses
- respective
- yonder

NOTICE: Photocopying any part of this book is forbidden by law.

Go On 311

Session 2

Notes

"Old Joe and the Carpenter"

Session 2

Notes

"Old Joe and the Carpenter"

STOP

27 In the chart below, show when the farmers' friendship changes, and why. Use details from "Old Joe and the Carpenter" in your answer.

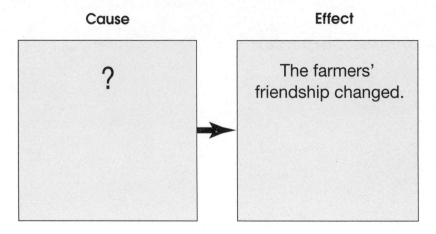

Cause   Effect

?   The farmers' friendship changed.

28 How does the carpenter defy Old Joe, and why? Use information from the story to support your answer.

_____

_____

_____

_____

_____

_____

29 What kind of characters are the farmers, and how do they affect the events of the story? Use examples from the story to support your answer.

_____

_____

_____

_____

_____

_____

Planning Page

You may PLAN your writing for Number 30 here if you wish, but do NOT write your final answer on this page. Your writing on this Planning Page will NOT count toward your final score. Write your final answer on Pages 316 and 317.

30 Explain how the events and theme of the story might differ if the carpenter had chosen to act differently. Use evidence from the story to support your answer.

Be sure to include:

- the main events of the story you heard
- the theme of the story you heard
- the events that might change
- the way the theme might change

 Check your writing for correct spelling, grammar, and punctuation.

_____

_____

_____

_____

_____

_____

_____

_____

_____

_____

_____

_____

Session 2

STOP

English Language Arts
BOOK 3

Session 3

Reading

*D*irections

In this part of the test, you are going to read an article called "Do Cats Really Have Nine Lives? and a poem called "The Kitten and the Falling Leaves." You will answer some questions and write about what you have read. You may look back at the articles as often as you like.

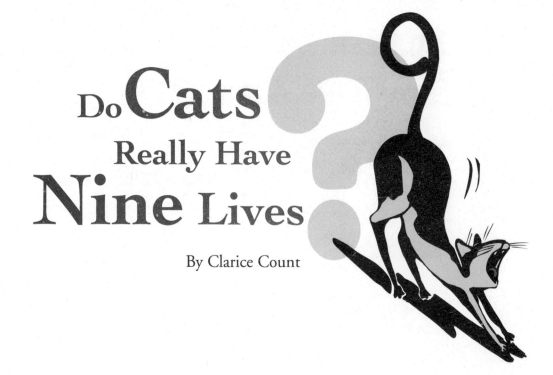

Do Cats Really Have Nine Lives?

By Clarice Count

H ave you ever heard the saying, "Cats have nine lives"? Think it's true? Well, it's not. It's one of the many myths "dogging" cats.

Myths have long followed cats, mostly because these animals have extraordinary abilities. Long ago, for example, people noticed that cats could survive falls with few, if any, injuries—even when they fell from really high places. Because cats, unlike humans, could fall from high places and survive, people began to get the idea that they were cheating death, or had nine lives. Some still think that.

It's also a myth that cats always land on their feet. Some cats do get injured falling—or jumping—from balconies, window sills, or rooftops. But they'll continue jumping. Why? Because, in general, they don't fear heights. When they're on the prowl, they're often more focused on catching birds or butterflies than on looking where they're leaping.

Cats have distinct advantages when falling. They're generally small animals, and weigh very little. Therefore, when they fall, they have little mass. They don't fall as fast as heavier animals—and, to some degree, they don't hit as hard. More important, though, is their above-average coordination and balance. When cats fall, they first determine which way is up. Then, they turn their heads in that direction and bring their front legs in to protect their faces from the impact. Next, the cats' reflexes kick in. Cats instinctively prepare themselves for landing by righting themselves in midair, just before impact.

Sometimes, the most dramatic falls are the least dangerous for cats. This only adds to the "nine lives" myth, though. A study done by New York veterinarians showed that the farther a fall, the less likely it is to be fatal for a cat. At a certain point—after about five stories or so—a falling cat reaches terminal velocity, meaning it stops falling faster and falls at a constant rate. After that, the longer a cat falls, the more time it has to prepare for landing, and the better its chance of going on to its "next life."

31 Why isn't it true that cats have nine lives? Use information from "Do Cats Really Have Nine Lives?" to support your answer.

_____

_____

_____

_____

_____

The Kitten and the Falling Leaves

By William Wordsworth

See the Kitten on the wall,
Sporting with the leaves that fall,
Withered leaves—one—two—and three,
From the lofty Elder-tree!
Through the calm and frosty air,
Of this morning bright and fair . . .
But the Kitten, how she starts;
Crouches, stretches, paws, and darts!
First at one, and then its fellow,
Just as light and just as yellow;
There are many now—now one—
Now they stop and there are none
What intenseness of desire,
In her upward eye of fire!
With a tiger-leap halfway,
Now she meets the coming prey,
Lets it go as fast, and then,
Has it in her power again:
Now she works with three or four,
Like an Indian Conjuror*;
Quick as he in feats of art,
Far beyond in joy of heart.

*magician

Session 3

32 How does the author use rhyme and meter in "The Kitten and the Falling Leaves"? Use examples from the poem to support your answer.

_____

_____

_____

_____

_____

33 How do the details and wording of the poem remind the reader of a real cat? Use details from both passages to support your answer.

_____

_____

_____

_____

_____

_____

Go On

Planning Page

You may PLAN your writing for Number 34 here if you wish, but do NOT write your final answer on this page. Your writing on this Planning Page will NOT count toward your final score. Write your final answer on Pages 325 and 326.

34 Explain how the article "Do Cats Really Have Nine Lives?" might be different if it were about an imaginary cat like the one in "The Kitten and the Falling Leaves." Use the article and the poem to support your answer.

Be sure to include:

- what the current passage is like
- how the passage would change with an imaginary character
- description of the imaginary character
- other important information, like plot and setting
- details from the story and poem

 Check your writing for correct spelling, grammar, and punctuation.

_____

_____

_____

_____

_____

_____

_____

_____

_____

_____

_____

Go On

Glossary

argument—the position an author takes for or against a subject and why

bibliographic information—alphabetical list of sources at the end of an essay or a paper

capitalization—use of capital letters in certain places to make writing clearer and reading faster

characters—people, animals, or other figures in a story

chart—illustration that shows information by putting data into geometric shapes; can show cause-and-effect or organizational relationships

clause—group of words that contains a subject and predicate and that functions as part of a complex or compound sentence

climax—point at which a story's main character must decide how to address the conflict

colon—punctuation mark used to introduce things; usually comes before an explanation of, or details about, the information before it

comma—punctuation mark that generally adds a pause in a sentence

complex sentence—sentence with two clauses, one of which is dependent

compound sentence—two or more simple sentences put together

conclusion—part of writing that wraps up the writing and restates any major points

conflict—main problem facing a story's main character(s); usually introduced at the beginning of a story

conjunction—a word that connects clauses or words

context—the words and sentences in a piece of writing that give meaning to other parts of the writing

dialect—how characters from a particular regional or social group speak

diction—the words authors or characters choose and how they use them

dependent clause—a clause that does not express a complete thought; also called a subordinate clause (see following entry)

drama—writing that is meant to be acted out using setting notes, stage directions, and dialogue

editorial—a type of writing that expresses opinions or reactions to news or events; much like "letter to the editor" (following entry)

essential information—information that connects to a story or point directly

exclamation point—punctuation mark that ends a sentence to express strong emotion, like excitement

fact—something that can be proven and is, therefore, always true

fiction—stories that use sentences and paragraphs to describe imaginary characters and events

figurative language—groups of words that express a special meaning; common examples are metaphors and similes

first-person perspective—the personal ("I," "we," or "us") point of view where the narrator is a character in the story and the reader's knowledge of the story is limited to the narrator's personal perspective

foreshadowing—literary device that hints at the events coming in a story

graph—type of illustration that shows how two or more things relate; common type is the bar graph

graphic organizer—set of connected boxes or circles that help visually relate ideas

haiku—very old type of Japanese poetry that has only three lines and 17 syllables

homophones—words that sound alike but are spelled differently (like "threw" and "through")

independent clause—clause that expresses a complete thought and could be its own sentence

index—information at the back of a publication, with detailed subjects and corresponding page numbers

inference—conclusion made based on information the reader has

introductory paragraph—beginning part of a piece of writing, designed to interest readers and explain topics

irony—literary device in which authors write one thing but mean another, make unexpected things happen, or tell readers what the characters do not know

lead—beginning sentence of a newspaper article that includes the "5 Ws and 1 H": *who, what, where, when, why,* and *how*

letter to the editor—type of writing that expresses opinions or reactions to news or events; much like "editorial"

magazine—information resource designed to inform and entertain

main idea—what a piece of writing is mostly about

map—illustration that show things like physical locations, how resources are distributed, and how to get from place to place

metaphor—literary device that compares two different things without using "like" or "as"; often uses a version of the verb "to be" (like "is")

meter—pattern of rhythm in poetry

narrator—author or character telling a story

newspaper—information resource that provides facts about current events

nonessential information—information that is unimportant to a story

nonfiction—stories that use sentences and paragraphs to describe real characters and events

noun-verb agreement—act of using the right verb for the subject

opinion—personal belief that cannot be proven and varies from individual to individual

period—most common punctuation mark that comes at the end of a sentence to show where the sentence stops

plot—what happens in a story; four main parts include conflict, rising action, climax, and resolution

poetry—type of writing that groups lines into stanzas and that uses expressive language, rhythm, and sometimes rhyme to communicate feelings

point of view—perspective of a story; the perspective of the narrator

predicate—group of words that describe something the subject is or does

proofreading—process of looking for spelling, capitalization, punctuation, verb-agreement, and formatting errors in a piece of writing

question mark—punctuation mark that ends a sentence to show uncertainty

resolution—way in which a story's main character solves the story's conflict

review—piece of writing that both describes a piece of work—such as a book or a film—and how the reader or viewer felt about that piece of work

reviewing—process of reading a piece of writing for content and understanding

revising—process of changing a piece of writing

rising action—events in a story after the conflict but before the climax; usually most of a story

rhythm—way in which lines of poetry sound when read aloud

rhyme—to sound alike

semicolon—punctuation mark that joins two independent clauses without a conjunction or that separates series items that have commas; like an extra-strength comma

setting—time and place in which a story occurs

simile—literary device that compares two different things using the words "like" or "as"

simple sentence—most basic kind of sentence; expresses just one thought and has just one subject and just one predicate

stage directions—writing in a piece of drama that tells when and where the drama is taking place and what the actors should do before, during, and after they speak

subject—part of a sentence that tells who or what the sentence is about

subordinate clause—clause that does not express a complete thought; also called a dependent clause

symbolism—literary device that uses one, usually concrete, thing to stand for another, usually abstract, thing

table of contents—part of a publication that lists the main subdivisions of a publication, as well as the pages on which those subdivisions start

textbook—resource that is designed to teach by providing nonfiction (see preceding entry) types of information

theme—central idea of a piece of writing

thesis statement—sentence that explains the main point of a piece of writing and its structure

third-person perspective—point of view of a story of someone not involved in the story; point of view in which the narrator is not a character

title—set of words that tells the general topic of a piece of writing

Scoring Rubric
for Short-Response Questions

Score	To get this score, you—
5	• discussed the correct element of the passage • interpreted the passage thoroughly • made connections beyond the text, if possible • developed your ideas fully • used relevant and accurate examples from the passage
4	• discussed the important elements of the passage • analyzed the passage literally • made connections beyond the text, if possible • gave an answer long enough to answer the question • gave some examples and details from the passage • may have included some mistakes
3	• answered the question partially • discussed the important elements of the passage incompletely • showed gaps in understanding of the passage • made some connections • gave a short answer • did not give enough examples from the text • may have included some mistakes
2	• answered the question partially • showed that you noticed important points but did not discuss them • did not show understanding of the whole passage • did not make connections beyond the passage • gave few examples • may have included some mistakes
1	• did not do what the question asked you to do • dealt with little of the actual passage • did not show that you understood the passage • made no connections beyond the passage • gave almost no examples, or none • made mistakes in fact or grammar
0	• gave an answer that made no sense at all.

NOTICE: Photocopying any part of this book is forbidden by law.

331

Scoring Rubric
for Extended-Response Questions

Score	To get this score, you—
5	• discussed the correct element of the passage • interpreted the passage thoroughly • made connections beyond the text, if possible • developed your ideas fully • used relevant and accurate examples from the passage • established and kept a clear focus • showed a logical sequence of ideas through the use of appropriate transitions or other devices • wrote an answer that was easy to read • used different kinds of sentences and good vocabulary
4	• discussed the important elements of the passage • analyzed the passage literally • made connections beyond the text, if possible • gave an answer long enough to answer the question • gave some examples and details from the passage • gave a focused answer, with some irrelevant details • showed an attempt at organization • wrote a readable response • used simple sentences and basic vocabulary • may have included some mistakes
3	• answered the question partially • discussed the important elements of the passage incompletely • showed gaps in understanding of the passage • made some connections • gave a short answer • did not give enough examples from the text • may have included some mistakes • gave a fairly focused answer, but may have wandered off the topic • attempted to organize your answer • wrote a readable reponse • used simple sentences and basic vocabulary

Scoring Rubric for Extended-Response Questions

(Continued)

Score	To get this score, you—
2	• answered the question partially • showed that you noticed important points but did not discuss them • did not show understanding of the whole passage • did not make connections beyond the passage • gave few examples • may have included some mistakes • showed an attempt to focus the answer • may have included some unimportant information • did not organize the answer very effectively • wrote a readable but very dull answer • used little vocabulary • did not organize thoughts well
1	• did not do what the question asked you to do • dealt with little of the actual passage • did not show that you understood the passage • made no connections beyond the passage • gave almost no examples, or none • made mistakes with facts or grammar • did not try to establish a focus • focused on minor details or unimportant information • showed little attempt at organization • gave an answer that was difficult to read • used little vocabulary • did not focus your thoughts
0	• gave an answer that was illegible or completely off topic

Common Student Errors

Frequently Misspelled Words	
Proper Spelling	**Common Misspellings**
ability	abilaty, abilety
about	abot, abowt
achieve	acheive
action	akshun, actoin
address	adres, addres, adress
again	agin, agan, agian
although	allthough, althuogh, althoh
always	allways, alwayze, alweys, alweeze
because	becuz, becase, becuase
bought	bawt, buoght, boght
calendar	calendir, calender, celendar, celindir
certain	serten, sirtin, certin, certain
children	chilldrun, childrin, childron, childrun
choose	chose, chews, chewz
color	culur, coler, colar, colir
could	cud, cood
doctor	ductor, docter, doctar, doctir, dacter
enough	enuf, enuff, enogh, enough
explain	esplane, esplain, explian, explane
favorite	favrit, faverite, favirite
friend	frend, friend
government	guvermint, goverment, govamint
great	grate, gret, grat
half	haf, hafl
hour	ar, are, ower, our
house	hows, huose
illustrate	illastrate, illastrait, ilustrate
instead	insted, insteed, innsted, instead
laugh	laff, luagh
listen	lissn, lissen, listin, lissin
loose	lose, lews, lows, loows

| More Frequently Misspelled Words ||
Proper Spelling	Common Misspellings
maybe	maybee, mebee, mabe, maby
muscle	mussul, mussel, mucsle, mussel
o'clock	oclock, aclock, a'clock
often	ofen, offin, oftin
occasion	ocassion, occasion, occasion
opposite	oposite, opossite, aposite
patient	payshunt, pateint, patent
people	peeple, poeple
quiet	quit, kwiet, queit
raise	raze, race, rayz, riase
receive	recieve, receeve, reseev, reseeve
recreation	recration, reckreation, recreatoin
read	reed, red
school	skool, schol, skuhool
said	sed, sayd, siad, sedd
since	sinse, sinze, scents, cinse, cinz
thought	thawt, thuoght, though

Commonly Confused Words	
accept (agree or receive)	except (but)
advise (to give advice)	advice (suggestion)
affect (to influence)	effect (result)
angel (heavenly being)	angle (slant)
capital (money)	capitol (gov't center)
its (belongs to it)	it's (it is)
lead (to guide)	led (past tense of "to lead")
lose (to not win)	loose (not tight)
principle (rule)	principal (heads the school)
right (correct; direction)	write (make letters)
sole (bottom of your foot)	soul (spirit)
there (a place)	their (belongs to them)
your (belongs to you)	you're (you are)

Reading List

Title	Author
Powwow	Ancona, George
Incredible Journey	Burnford, Sheila
The Landry News	Clements, Andrew
Gregor the Overlander	Collins, Susan
Arthur: The Seeing Stone	Cossley-Holland, Kevin
The Midwife's Apprentice	Cushman, Karen
Because of Winn-Dixie	DiCamillo, Kate
The Diary of a Young Girl	Frank, Anne
Lincoln: A Photobiography	Freedman, Russell
The Gorillas of Gill Park	Gordon, Amy
Sweet Whispers, Brother Rush	Hamilton, Virginia
The Birthday Room	Henkes, Kevin
The "Nancy Drew" Series	Keene, Carolyn
Regarding the Fountain	Klise, Kate
Rabbit Hill	Lawson, Robert
Family Pictures-Cuadros de Familia	Lomas Garza, Carmen
The Dragon of Lonely Island	Rupp, Rebecca
Straw Into Gold	Schmidt, Gary D.
Squids Will Be Squids	Scieszka, Jon
Staples	Shabanu, Suzanne
It's Disgusting and We Ate It	Solheim, James
Baseball in April and Other Stories	Soto, Gary
The Bones in the Cliff	Stevenson, James
Roll of Thunder, Hear My Cry	Taylor, Mildred D.
Maizon at Blue Hill	Woodson, Jacqueline
The Pigman	Zindel, Paul